WITNESS TO THE EXECUTION:
The Odyssey of Amelia Earhart

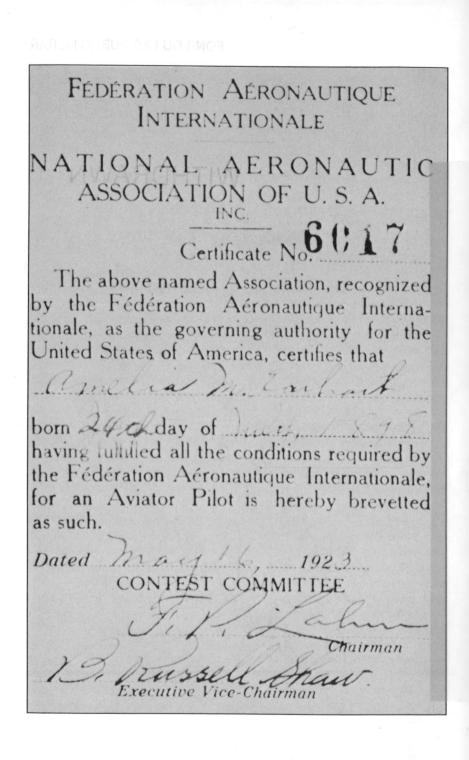

FÉDÉRATION AÉRONAUTIQUE
INTERNATIONALE

NATIONAL AERONAUTIC
ASSOCIATION OF U. S. A.
INC.

Certificate No. **6017**

The above named Association, recognized by the Fédération Aéronautique Internationale, as the governing authority for the United States of America, certifies that

Amelia M. Earhart

born *24th* day of *July 1 8 9 8* having fulfilled all the conditions required by the Fédération Aéronautique Internationale, for an Aviator Pilot is hereby brevetted as such.

Dated *May 16*, 192*3*

CONTEST COMMITTEE

F. R. Lahm
Chairman

D. Russell Shaw.
Executive Vice-Chairman

WITNESS TO THE EXECUTION

The Odyssey of Amelia Earhart

T.C. BUDDY BRENNAN

RENAISSANCE
HOUSE

A Division of Jende-Hagan, Inc.
541 Oak Street • P.O. Box 177
Frederick, CO 80530

RENAISSANCE HOUSE PUBLISHERS
541 Oak Street ~ P.O. Box 177
Frederick, Colorado 80530

Written by Ray Rosenbaum

Frontispiece: Pilot's license issued to Amelia Earhart on May 16, 1923.

Cover photo of Amelia Earhart as it appeared on her 1923 pilot's license.

**A home video based on *WITNESS TO THE EXECU-
TION* and incorporating many of Brennan's interviews with the islanders was produced by the Experi-
mental Aircraft Association. Videos may be pur-
chased by calling this toll free number: 1-800-521-
9221.**

Library of Congress Cataloging in Publication Data

Brennan, T.C. Buddy, 1924-
    Witness to the execution.

        "Written by Ray Rosenbaum"--T.p. verso.
        Bibliography: p.
        Includes index.
        1. Earhart, Amelia, 1897-1937.   2. Aeronautics--Flights.
I. Rosenbaum, Ray.   II. Title.
TL540.E3B68   1988   629.13'092'4   [B]   88-18358
ISBN 1-55838-107-4
ISBN 1-55838-108-2 (pbk.)

Introduction

Witness to the Execution recounts my search to determine the fate of a woman who never knew me, a woman I never met. A pert, tousel-haired tomboy with remarkable courage, she vanished under tragic circumstances the morning of July 2, 1937 while attempting a record-setting flight around the world. What *actually* happened that morning has become a 50-year enigma.

I became involved in this fascinating saga almost by accident. During 1981 I was in the Marshall Islands attempting to salvage Japanese warplanes abandoned there after World War II. Remarks by the native islanders implying that Amelia Earhart had crashed nearby changed the entire focus of my search. Almost overnight I was drawn into the mystery, and have since spent more than five years attempting to unravel the maze of rumor, conjecture and misinformation surrounding her disappearance. I believe I am now able to make a significant contribution to that sketchy hoard of knowledge garnered during the past half century. My evidence is not of a forensic nature that would permit the case to be stamped "forever closed." Mine is believable circumstantial evidence, a compilation of documented eyewitness testimony, physical evidence and logical deduction that withstands the most critical examination. You, the reader, must be the judge of its worth.

Whenever possible I develop my story through the eyes of people who possess firsthand knowledge of events. Many of these conversations involve a translator, others are with people whose command of English is limited. Not all would agree to appear on video tape. I have paraphrased and edited conversations when necessary for clarity and continuity of the narrative, but the content in each case remains factual.

I am under no illusion that my story will change the course of history or that it will become a reference text for future scholars. It is a story of one man's trip into the past, an insight into an era which spanned the period after the Great Depression through World War II.

It is my intention to return to Saipan to conduct a full-scale archeological dig, with experts from a variety of fields as part of the team. Before such an expedition can be undertaken, however, we must be assured of the support and cooperation of the islanders involved, to insure that we have the time and facilities to conduct the excavation properly.

In the meantime, I would welcome relevant information that readers might have which would assist us in coming closer to determining the fate of Amelia Earhart and Fred Noonan. I urge you to write me in care of Renaissance House Publishers; P.O. Box 177; Frederick, Colorado 80530.

Buddy Brennan
Houston, Texas
1988

Acknowledgement is given to my friend Ray Rosenbaum for his work in translating my research into book form.

Foreword

More than 50 years have now passed since Amelia Earhart departed from Lae and flew off into the unknown. Her disappearance is certainly the single greatest aviation mystery and may even be the single most perplexing mystery of all time. Periodically, references are made to the Bermuda Triangle and its mysterious connections, but even that is insignificant in comparison to the continued interest in Amelia Earhart, her flight and what "really happened." The degree of interest is particularly curious when you realize that Amelia was only in evidence about 10 years. In that short period she left an indelible mark on the world that no one has even come close to equalling.

We Ninety-Nines honor Amelia's memory by calling our scholarship fund the Amelia Earhart Memorial Scholarship Fund. We own her birthplace homestead in Atchison, Kansas and each year we enshrine greats and near greats in our Forest of Friendship. The airport in Atchison is the Amelia Earhart Airport and the football stadium is also named in her honor. Many schools, a mountain, numerous streets, luggage, and a portion of the highway leading into Atchison are named for her. Painters have done her picture; sculptors her bust and statues. There have been songs and poetry written in her memory. She is certainly my hero.

Amelia Earhart was the first president of the Ninety-Nines, Inc., an international organization of women pilots. We now have members in 33 countries and are approximately 7,000 strong. I am sure the 7,000 have at least that many ideas of "what really happened." But after fifty years, I don't suppose it matters what "really happened." Most of the players are gone now, save Muriel Morrissey and her family. What does matter is the impact Amelia had on the world then and continues to have even now. Her spirit still lives in all of us who dream or aspire. She is a great role model today, just as she was before her last flight. She inspires those who fail to keep trying, and those who succeed to go even further. We will dream our dreams because she did. We will try because she tried, and when we fail we know that failure is just one step toward ultimate success. She will be forever there, beckoning us to take that extra step, walk that extra mile, give that extra bit of effort and thus live our lives to the fullest.

Our international headquarters in Oklahoma City has many books, each written by someone who is sure he or she has the answer, but the only things *we* know for sure are that she was our first president and that she was lost on her around-the-world flight. Buddy Brennan's book gives you the feeling that you are right there exploring, and suffering the frustrations when things don't go well. I have viewed his video tape taken on trip IV. The people on the tape are convincing, and you find yourself wanting to believe that Buddy is on the right track. Buddy brings the whole adventure into your home as if you are personally discussing the trip. The story rings so true you have the itch to go with him on his next journey to Saipan in the hope of being there when the mystery is brought to its ultimate conclusion.

Hazel H. Jones,
International President
The Ninety-Nines, 1984-86

Chapter One:

THE FIRST EXPEDITION

"**Y**ou want old airplane, you find airplane American lady crash in." The words were accompanied by a shy smile. I was talking with Mr. Tanaki, one of the more interesting native inhabitants of the little Marshall island of Majuro. He spoke English quite well but his speech was slightly blurred, the result of a mild stroke some years previous. Operator of the heavy equipment yard, he was intelligent and articulate, despite the slight speech impairment.

I considered his words with scant interest. This wasn't the first time I had heard gossip about a white woman and man appearing on the island before World War II. They had been arrested as spies by the Japanese Army and disappeared. Further gossip claimed that "Tokyo Rosa"* was Amelia Earhart; the man was Fred Noonan, her navigator. Earhart had gone down somewhere in the Pacific on an attempted flight around the world, I recalled, but it had been a long way from here.

I regarded him with open skepticism. "Mr. Tanaki," I said with attempted humor, "that happened more than 40 years ago. How can you be so sure? You couldn't have been more than a child."

His eyes twinkled from behind thick glasses. "I am 63 years old, Mr. Brennan. I worked for company suppling coal to Japanese Navy at the time. One night I was working at refueling the *Koshu*. My friend was part of the crew and I was talking to him. An officer came up to us. He said to stop

---

* Japanese name for American Spy Lady

refueling. The ship was going to sail right away.

"Ship was gone about a week. When it came back, I ask my friend where they went in so much hurry. He would not tell me. They could not tell anyone about the trip. Finally he tells me--they went to search for American airplane that crashed."

"I've heard that tale Mr. Tanaki," I said, mildly disappointed. "I'm afraid finding that one is out of the question."

"Maybe. Other men from America, they come here, oh, several times. They don't find. It still out there, someplace." Those last two simple sentences were to turn my life upside down for the next five years. They were to transform a middle-aged Houston, Texas businessman into a combination investigator, explorer, and amateur archeologist. Four more times I would return to this idyllic tropical paradise, each time equipped with more and better equipment and advisors--and a growing dent in my bank account.

I had made this trip to the Marshall Islands in search of World War II era Japanese war planes. Many had been abandoned, I was told, on the nearby island of Mili Mili in 1944, ahead of advancing American forces. It was my intention to obtain one or more for the Confederate Air Force or an interested museum.

The planes were there in profusion, but the ones we examined were badly deteriorated. In addition, the ever-encroaching jungle had almost succeeded in devouring its alien visitors. Most planes could be reached only with the assistance of sweating machete teams. Reclamation was possible but far from easy. With dampened spirits, my long time friend, Dick Huntoon, and I returned to the island of Majuro. I decided to spend the rest of our stay visiting with the friendly islanders.

Thanking Tanaki for his suggestion, I returned to my quarters. The trip had been a complete failure as far as I was concerned. I eyed my room in disgust--Le Grande Hotel Eastern Gateway--a pile of concrete cubicles. Asthmatic air conditioners perched in each window wheezed a losing battle with the humid heat. I retrieved my bottle of drinking water, examined the single chair for cockroaches, and sat down to ruminate.

Another full day lay ahead before we could claim our seats on Air Micronesia and start the long trip home. With any luck they wouldn't be carrying livestock this trip! I looked at my watch--three o'clock--another two hours before the water would be turned on. Then I would have, at best, a couple hours to take a shower before the precious stuff was turned off again for the day. I looked forward to this brief respite. Tramping through that jungle on Mili had been hot work.

My first question as the machete team started opening a path had concerned snakes. The place looked like python heaven! Oh no, I was told cheerfully, no snakes. The mongoose takes care of that. What they didn't mention were the palm rats, which were *everywhere*! One of the old Zeros we investigated was apparently their Hilton.

We ate a solitary dinner and turned in early, but sleep eluded me. Tanaki's words kept returning. A world-famous person might lie in an unmarked grave only miles from here. The thought sent a tingle up my spine. The history buff in me was intrigued. And her airplane; what a find that would be!

I slipped on trousers and a pair of sandals. The thought of that white sand beach in the moonlight was irresistible. The village was dark and quiet as I made my way toward the gentle murmur of the surf. In the distance, lightning flickered with varying hues of crimson against the ever-present cumulus. A gaggle of night birds set up a raucous quarrel, blocking the whisper of breezes in the huge palm trees.

I found a fallen palm trunk, sat down and lit a cigarette. The thought of our impending departure from this peaceful corner of the earth depressing. "Watch it Brennan," I laughed to myself. Tanaki's words continued to plague me, and I sat there a long time.

When I finally returned to my room sleep came easily. My mind was made up--I was coming back to this place. I would find that airplane! The entire U. S. Navy hadn't been able to find it, so what made me think I could? It presented a challenge I couldn't resist.

Next morning, my blue funk of the previous afternoon gone, I laid plans for the day. I was determined to run down these Earhart rumors. The old man's words yesterday seemed to imply some special knowledge. But how much could I believe of what he told me? Was he just indulging in that age-old sport of stringing along the American visitor? He was old; was this one of those things he had told so often he now believed it himself?

I set out in search of Ben Berry. What Ben didn't know about the island gossip he could find out. He was the Fixer Supreme of Majuro and the entire Marshalls group as far as I could tell. If you had to make an urgent telephone call, Ben could place you at the head of the waiting line. Need to meet a government official or a member of the Royal Family? No problem; Ben could arrange it. Ben had adopted me upon my arrival at Majuro. A transplanted Texan from Beaumont, perhaps he felt a special kinship for another Texan. Transportation, scuba divers, machete teams, a chartered airplane appeared as if by magic.

Plying Ben with a cold can of Schlitz, we retired to a remote corner of his favorite bar. "Ben," I asked, "What do you know about the story of Amelia Earhart crashing around here?"

Ben shrugged. "Oh, I hear it. The older ones talk about it some, even yet. The younger ones; they don't seem to know or care much about the story. It *was* a long time ago. Some white man and woman were prisoners of the Japs here before the war started, but who knows whether it was Earhart?"

"Well I was talking to the old man, Tanaki, yesterday and he told me a story about it. If that airplane is around these islands, I'd give anything to find it. It'd be a lot bigger find than those Zeros I came after."

"A lot of people have been out here looking for it I understand, before my time I guess. I think they gave up."

"But I was impressed with the old man. I got the feeling he wanted to tell me more but didn't. What's his reputation on the island?"

"Oh pretty good, as far as I know. You want to talk to

someone who can tell you for sure?"

"Who would that be?"

Ben grinned. "How about a federal judge?"

"You mean it?"

"Sure. Judge Kabua Kabua. Knows everything about everyone in the islands. I can fix it up for you, easy."

He did, with the true Berry magic. Soon we were pulling up in front of Judge Kabua Kabua's house, but not until Ben had taken me back to the hotel to change from my walking shorts into long trousers. Seems you don't show up on official business here wearing shorts. I noticed that Ben was not wearing socks, just the rubber thong sandals favored everywhere in the islands, but at least he was wearing long trousers!

That Judge Kabua was a man of some affluence was borne out by the three rusting automobile carcasses in front. In a land where the maximum life of a car is three years, they are abandoned in front of one's house. The more cars one abandons, the wealthier one is.

The favorite position for informal conversation in the islands is squatting out of doors. I did my best and listened as Ben explained to the judge that I was interested in Mr. Tanaki's story about the search for a downed American plane in 1937. The old judge assured me gravely that Mr. Tanaki was an honorable man. His word could be trusted.

In response to questions about any other persons who might shed some light on the incident, he became evasive. It was a long time ago. He, personally, had no recollection of the matter. The thing happened someplace else. The white man and woman did not come to the island of Majuro. I was getting the American tourist treatment.

Back in the car I questioned Ben. Who else on the island could I talk to and get some straight answers? Now Ben became evasive. It was only after we returned to the bar and settled behind another can of Schlitz that he began to talk freely.

"Are you serious about trying to find out what happened to Earhart's airplane?" he began.

I assured him I was; not only serious but determined.

"Okay. There are people that can help you. I can't say they will though."

"Why not, for heaven's sake? This thing happened more than 40 years ago."

"Mr. Brennan, you're a nice guy. I hope you don't get mad at what I'm going to say."

I assured him I was ready to listen.

"You see, a lot of people on the islands don't really think much of Americans."

I was astounded. "Not like the Americans? Good God, we liberated these islands from the Japanese! They became free people because of us. A lot of American GI blood went into that effort!"

"Well, I'm only telling you, there are those who don't think we did them any favor. Things are pretty bad around here now--no jobs, the economy is a mess. Look around you; the kids have nothing to do, nothing to look forward to. We built schools, gave them skill training; then nothing. Those who can't get away shoot pool and drink American beer all day. The only good jobs are with the government, and those are filled by people who show no indication of making room for the younger ones.

"Sure, we poured money in here at first--$600-800 per person per year. This to a people who existed on bartering copra, shells and the like for cloth and staples. Then we proceeded to blow hell out of Bikini and Eniwetok; spread radiation that still isn't cleaned up. No, they'll be nice to you, but don't expect a ticker tape parade."

I was still stunned. "I appreciate your telling me all this Ben, but how am I supposed to approach this thing? How can I convince them I'm a respectable guy looking for help? Nothing they tell me can hurt them after all this time. Would it help if I advertised in the paper; asked for leads; offered rewards?"

"That's probably the *worst* thing you could do, Mr. Brennan. Play it by ear. Don't rush things. Times are changing; you just might get lucky. Now, would you like to have a meeting with the President?" Ben had reverted to his Mr. Fixit role.

As I learned more about the local political and social structure, I would find that someone's permission is required for just about anything on the islands. President Kabua's endorsement would open many doors. We had a brief but pleasant visit, and I found the President to be a highly intelligent and perceptive man. He promised full cooperation, but explained that government archives, as such, did not extend back that far. He personally had no knowledge which could help me but suggested I visit with Mr. Bilamon Amaron. Mr. Amaron supposedly treated the two American prisoners when he worked for a Japanese dispensary on the island of Jaluit, a short distance southwest. My spirits soared. I hadn't imagined things would be this easy! My search was less than one day old and I was going to talk with a man who perhaps actually saw Earhart and Noonan alive!

Just as quickly as they had risen, my hopes were dashed. Amaron either could not be found or would not talk with me. My time was up, but I had enough evidence to convince me I was on the right track. I boarded the outbound plane full of plans and enthusiasm, and wanting in the worst way to find that airplane. Indeed, I *was* going to find that airplane.

During our layover in Honolulu I found a copy of Fred Goerner's book *The Search For Amelia Earhart*. The long overwater leg to Los Angles passed in a blur as I buried myself in his account of the event. I almost missed my flight to Houston running down another Earhart book, *Amelia Earhart Lives*, by Joe Klaas and Joe Gervais.

By the time we deplaned in Houston I had read two "authoritative and documented" versions of Earhart's last flight. They couldn't have been more contradictory! One version has them killed under vaguely defined circumstances somewhere in the Marshalls. The other has them returned to the United States as part of a secret deal with Japan. "How," I asked myself, "could two people writing from similiar documentation draw such conflicting conclusions?" And theirs were not the only two theories on the topic.

I was impressed with the depth of Goerner's research. But Joe Gervais and others in his book were experienced pilots; they had flown in the area of Amelia's disappearance. Frankly my determination started to wane. I hadn't realized how many people or man-hours this business had already involved.

Still, Mr. Tanaki's words kept coming back. "They don't find. It still out there somewhere." In the end it was tenacity, not superior investigative skills, that led me to some startling new answers to the 50+-year enigma surrounding the fate of Amelia Earhart.

Queen and Mayor of Mili

Dick Huntoon

President Kabua,
Republic of Marshall Islands

Chapter Two:

FROM THE VIEWPOINT OF DICK HUNTOON

A mutual passion for golf, small stakes gin rummy and tacos *el carbon* has cemented a close friendship between myself and Dick Huntoon. It was Dick that I had cajoled into making that first expedition with me, but he hadn't needed much encouragement:

During the past 40 years, I've become accustomed to the unusual when Buddy's around. So I didn't think it strange when he asked if I wanted to go on a little trip with him. When I asked where, he simply replied, "Just be at the airport, 9:15, Sunday morning. Better pack a bag for about two weeks." When I insisted on knowing our destination he announced offhandedly, "We're going to the Marshall Islands, Majuro, to be specific."

I was immediately interested. The island of Majuro was a prominent historical landmark during World War II; our Navy used its lagoon as a safe harbor. Majuro was an R & R area for thousands of swabbies after months at sea. I had been a Navy carrier pilot during WW II but not in the Pacific. Naturally I wanted to visit this area where major naval battles had taken place and relive some of those headline-making events. I hurriedly rearranged business activities and joined Buddy on what proved to be the first step in a truly astounding saga.

Buddy explained that the purpose of our trip

was twofold. First, he had heard that the famous aviatrix of the 1930s, Amelia Earhart, might have crashed there. He was curious and wanted to do some "nosing around." Second, in typical Brennan style, he had come up with a scheme to pay our expenses. Supposedly old Japanese warplanes, abandoned ahead of our advancing troops, littered the atolls like so many coconuts. Buddy had been calling museums and private collectors and had, in a matter of hours, gotten commitments which could cover all our expenses if only we could retrieve these items for use as static displays. I was only too glad to help him.

I was dismayed when I stepped off the airplane that first afternoon on Majuro. After 13 hours in the air, dreaming about a tropical paradise, I just was not prepared for what greeted us. Palm trees were about equal in number to rusted Toyota and Datsun taxicabs. Thatched huts with dirt floors and walls made of old crating and salvaged aluminum stretched as far as the eye could see from the road, Majuro, incidentally, has 31 miles of road, running from one end, without interruption, to the other end. One terminus is Laura Beach, the other Rita Beach--names courtesy of the American Navy--Lauren Bacall and Rita Hayworth being their inspiration. A cab ride the entire distance costs ten cents.

The island was not a battleground during WW II. The Japanese evacuated ahead of our invasion fleet and we just walked ashore. You'd never know it. Enough rusting armaments, including unexploded bombs, shells and sea mines, exist to equip a respectable army. It appears that our troops abandoned almost as much material as the Japs when they departed. I stood on the beach amid rusting debris and tried to visualize the harbor at the height of our drive westward--ships of the line, immaculate in their gray paint; small craft scurrying to and fro like so many water beetles; momentous, heroic acts being planned and carried out. I

found this casual abandonment of tools which had
served us so well extremely depressing.

The airplanes we sought were reportedly concentrated on the island of Mili Mili, a major Japanese airbase located in the Mili Atoll some 45 minutes flying time to the south. We quickly made
charter arrangements. Time and some devastating
bombing on our part had taken their toll, but the
trip had its rewards. We were met by most of the
island's population, about 250 natives. Our first
stop was to be introduced to the Queen of Mili,
whose permission was necessary to prowl the
island. I was intrigued by the fact that even in this
primitive setting the old Queen managed to exude
a regal aura. She spoke no English but through our
interpreter conveyed her sanction for our search.
As ruler, she stood to receive a healthy cut of any
money spent on our search. I was curious about
reports that she had married the commander of
Japanese forces on the island, but refrained from
asking.

The Queen's brother, a giant of a man and a
true *National Geographic* representation of
Micronesia, invited us to his house, two miles away,
for tea. It was an elegant home by Mili standards;
the one room with   dirt floor housed his wife, five
small children and himself. After drinking the
vilest concoction I ever recall tasting, we expressed
our appreciation and left to begin our investigation.

One of the many people we talked with that
afternoon had an intriguing story. He remembered
an enterprising American P-38 pilot who would
land on the strip late at night and, executing a
tight circle, spray everything in sight with bursts
from his six wing-mounted 50-caliber machine
guns! It was most effective, but the Japanese were
not totally without initiative. After suffering a
number of these annoying invasions, they dug a
trench across the main runway and our hero's
landing came to an abrupt, ignominious end. The
disposition of the pilot is not known, but the re-

mains of the P-38, or at least *a* P-38, still lie in the jungle just off the old airstrip.

No sooner were we reestablished on Majuro than I found myself slipping into the easy life of the islands. The beaches, in spite of the litter, are enchanting and the water color indescribable. Here was Dick Huntoon, a normally active guy, spending more than two hours gazing out over nothing but an empty seascape! Majuro has an inescapable magic, as a number of fellow Americans have discovered. Among them are Grant Gordon, a reporter for the Majuro weekly newspaper, Tom Getty, owner of the Marshall Island Yacht Club (the name is just *slightly* pretentious), and a young couple from Laguna Beach, California. On a trip around the world in a 35-foot ketch, the pair had developed radio problems and put into Majuro for repairs--four months earlier.

Although I am not a true epicurean, a menu featuring powdered eggs, powdered milk and stale cheese tends to grow tiring. In desperation one evening I pleaded for the "best dish in the house." I was rewarded with a generous portion of raw tuna topped with slices of raw onions. It was then that I decided that powdered eggs and cheese *are* quite high in protein.

The Majuro people grow on you, especially the children. At times it seems the average age of Marshall Islanders must be about ten. They follow in droves, intensely interested in every move you make. Most speak English, but they are shy and it's nearly impossible to share their deeper thoughts.

Their elders are kind and helpful, despite occasional cool distrust of Americans. Radiation poisoning, for example, is something they just won't discuss. One small office bears a sign designating it "Headquarters for Radiation Litigation." Ironically the building bears a marked resemblance to other structures proclaiming the construction was "Funded by CIP (acronym for Capital Improvement Program) - U.S. Congress."

Our departure time approached all too rapidly. Buddy, momentarily depressed with his failure to obtain a shipload of antique airplanes, had developed a sudden inordinate interest in Amelia Earhart's disappearance. There was no question but what he would pursue it.

I took with me one cherished treasure--a gift for my wife. The necklace, given me by the wife of a Nahru Atoll Chieftain, promises to protect my home from advancing lava flows and disgruntled native warriors.

Meeting of licensed women pilots' organization,
November 2, 1929. Earhart is far left, back.

Third Annual
Annette Gipson
Air Race -
June, 1934.
Earhart is
second from
right.

Joanne Sartain

Amelia Earhart and
navigator Fred Noonan on
left are interviewed by
KGU radio in Honolulu in
1935

Chapter Three:
AMELIA:
THE OFFICIAL VERSION

I soon discovered that few shared my enthusiasm. A trip to recover Japanese warplanes that had obviously existed was one thing. But to pursue a mystery that people had investigated unsuccessfully for 50 years was something else again. My family was openly skeptical. My wife Evelyn, later one of my staunchest supporters, was the most vocal.

Knowing it was possible to obtain previously classified documents from government files under the Freedom Of Information Act, I contacted Texas Representative Jack Brooks for assistance. It was surprisingly easy. Shortly I was the owner of some 2,000 pages of old files which provided a complete picture of government involvement before and after Earhart's ill-fated attempt to fly around the world. Everything was there, from copies of Presidential memos to logs of ships involved in one of the decade's most extensive search efforts.

While awaiting this bonanza, I had read everything I could find on the subject. With the old records--the official sources--I figured I could discover what had *really* happened. I c'oseted myself for two days and most of the interveni·ng night, devouring every scrap of information in that bo·..

Down the center of a legal tablet I drew a line, heading left side "proven fact" and right side "conclusions and conjecture." Reviewing the results a few days later, I discovered the right side (conjecture) filled most of three pads while "Facts" ended about two thirds of the way through the first pad. I was surprised and disappointed with this imbalance but determined to construct my scenario from the "fact" side.

Amelia Earhart Putnam had gained considerable notoriety in the early '30s as an aviatrix. She was the first woman to cross the Atlantic and the first woman to fly nonstop from Mexico City to New York, captivating the American public with her exploits. Earhart had a pretty face, a trim figure and affected mannish clothing for flying, often wearing a silk scarf about the neckline. Her hair was modishly short. Earhart's husband, George Palmer Putnam of publishing fame, devoted full time to managing his wife's flying career.

In 1936, Amelia, then nearing 39, announced her intention to fly solo around the world--not along the northern latitudes, where the distance is shorter, but along an equatorial route. Radio navigational aids were just coming into use. Aircraft instrumentation was designed more for "contact" flying than for operations in inclement weather.

Earhart had conducted a series of seminars on flying at Purdue University, was well-liked there, and the school agreed to furnish a new airplane in the name of research for her proposed flight. The new Lockheed 10E, twin engine craft was a popular passenger transport, used widely around the world. Putnam arranged for Paul Mantz, noted stunt flyer and aircraft designer, to specifically equip the plane for around-the-world flight. Mantz would teach Amelia to fly the *Electra*, the largest airplane she had thus far attempted. On March 17, 1937, Amelia departed Oakland, California for Honolulu to begin the first leg of her journey.

Government support for the trip was considerable. Earlier, Amelia had requested air-to-air refueling from U.S. Navy planes and the Navy Department had conducted feasibility tests, pronouncing the plan viable. Although approved in principle, it was later dropped in favor of a landing at tiny Howland Island, some 2,000 miles southeast of Hawaii. The government constructed an airstrip there, expressly for refueling Earhart's plane. A Coast Guard cutter, the *Itasca*, was dispatched to stand off Howland and provide radio navigation assistance. Another Navy ship, the *Ontario*, was positioned about halfway between Howland and the island of New Guinea. American embassies around the world were alerted to do anything possible to support her passage.

The many preparations were thwarted when, on takeoff from Hawaii during her next leg, Amelia ground looped the *Electra*. The damage was substantial; the plane was shipped back to the United States where Paul Mantz undertook the task of rebuilding. Putnam vowed the effort would resume as soon as repairs were complete.

The airplane Amelia piloted the next time bore little resemblance to the one delivered by Lockheed less than a year before. Paul Mantz had ordered a larger version of the Pratt and Whitney engines installed. An internal fuel tank now filled most of the forward "passenger" compartment. A simple table and chair were installed for the navigator. All passenger section windows were covered except for one observation port for the navigator. Entrance and exit from the cockpit was through an overhead hatch which doubled as a window from which to take celestial fixes. An "R" was added to the plane's identification number after the standard "N" prefix to designate it a research aircraft.

State of the art air to ground radio equipment was installed. Voice communication was provided via two pre-tuned transmitting frequencies, 3105 and 6210 kc, with a hand-tuned receiver on standard medium range frequencies. An emergency set was also included, pre-tuned to 500 kc, the standard emergency frequency. For maximum range, a 300-foot "trailing wire antenna" was required. It consisted of antenna wire coiled on a reel with a heavy lead weight affixed, and could be cranked back inside the airplane when not in use, or for landing and takeoff.

The most useful navigating device was a direction finding radio with a loop antenna. It utilized the principle that no signal could be heard when radio waves were received simultaneously on all sides of a coiled wire antenna, for reception would be effectively canceled. Conversely when the coil or loop was rotated so that signals were received from the side, a maximum signal could be heard. The technique for use was to tune the station from an auxiliary (called a clothes line) antenna, then switch to the loop antenna, which resembled a large doughnut. When the "doughnut hole" faced the station, no signal could be heard, but when rotated to the side, a maximum strength signal was received. A plane to station bearing was obtained on the zero or "null" signal. The set operated in the low frequency range, hand-tuned from about 200 kc through the standard AM broadcast frequencies.

Records strongly indicate that Amelia removed the trailing wire antenna before departing the U.S., as a weight-saving measure. Another unconfirmed report indicates the clothes line antenna to the direction finding radio was disconnected. Also removed was an antenna "loading coil," essential to long range transmission, and the Morse signal sending key. (Neither Amelia or her navigator were proficient in Morse code.) Thus the flight commenced with less than half the full radio navigation capability.

Instructor Paul Mantz, navigator Harry Manning, and second navigator Fred Noonan accompanied Amelia on the first leg of the aborted westward departure. It was decided the second flight would be east-bound to take advantage of seasonal weather changes. Manning had taken a leave of absence from his job to make the first flight, but his leave had expired so it was Fred Noonan in the "tube" when Amelia broke ground from Miami June 1, 1937.

The flight proceeded eastward with only minor difficulties, one being the arrangement for communication between pilot and navigator. The internal fuel tank virtually blocked passage between the cockpit and passenger compartment. The solution was to suspend a fishing rod from tabs affixed to the ceiling, along which notes could be passed.

The most demanding leg of the journey would be the 2,550 miles from Lae, New Guinea to Howland Island. The first 600 miles crossed small islands of the Solomon group. The remaining distance, almost 2,000 miles, must be transited without reference to land. Less than 100 miles north of the flight path lurked unfriendly territory under Japanese jurisdiction.

In a time when radio nets were generally operated independent of one another, radio procedures were somewhat vague. The commercial airlines relied on their "company" frequencies; the U.S. Navy used another series; merchant ships yet another. Private aircraft such as Earhart's made their own arrangements. The only universal frequency was 500 kc, known as the emergency frequency. Records from the commander of the Coast Guard cutter *Itasca* reflect his annoyance at being unable to establish which frequencies would be used for what and when.

The crew and plane remained at Lae four days awaiting a favorable weather forecast and fine tuning the *Electra*. "Forecast" is an optimistic term for the meteorological conditions Earhart could expect to encounter. Regularly scheduled weather observations in that area were virtually nonexistent. Surface observations by shipping interests and Navy vessels were collected and analyzed for flight purposes on an "as required" basis. In Japanese territories, nothing reliable was usually available. The forecast upon which Earhart based her flight plan was preceded with a warning that it was only an estimate of conditions.

Departure was timed to permit visual reference to the Solomon Islands during daylight hours but late enough to insure a daytime arrival at Howland. Earhart provided Lae with hourly position reports for the first six hours of flight. After that, no officially recognized transmissions are recorded until initial contact with the *Itasca* some ten hours later. The *Itasca* was well prepared for her role in guiding Amelia to her destination. The crew was experienced and well briefed. A portable direction finding radio had been placed ashore at Howland. Lack of a flight-following capability and of pre-determined communication procedures was annoying but not critical.

Radio signals from KHAQQ (Earhart's radio call sign)

were picked up by the *Itasca* at 0345 GCT*, but satisfactory two-way communication was never established. Amelia gave indications of having received some *Itasca* transmissions but never clearly acknowledged that she understood the messages. The last recorded transmission from KHAQQ was at 2025 GCT. Shortly thereafter *Itasca* advised Honolulu that the flight was overdue Howland and presumed down. *Itasca* commenced a search that would involve five other major vessels: Navy ships *Lexington*, *Colorado*, *Lamson*, *Drayton*, and *Cushing*. More than 40 aircraft from the *Lexington* and *Colorado* were utilized. For 16 days this force searched the equivalent of a 500-mile square, but there was no evidence of the Earhart plane.

Two messages formed the grim parenthesis to a fruitless rescue effort. The first, a haunting: "I AM CIRCLING BUT CANNOT SEE YOU." The second, a terse "FROM: COMDESRON 2 - TO: COM 14 -- 0018 SEARCH TODAY SUNDAY COMPLETED AS SCHEDULED 1551."

No further official search would be conducted. The event was logged as a tragic accident. No investigation as to probable cause would be carried out. Scarcely 18 months later, George Palmer Putnam would request and obtain a certificate of death. Amelia Earhart Putnam, born July 24, 1898, was officially dead at age 39. But the chapter would not be closed that easily.

---

* Greenwich Civil Time

Amelia Earhart

Chapter Four:

THE SEARCH COMMENCES

A world famous aviatrix lost, and the official reaction? A figurative shrug of the shoulders. I pictured this event in the 1980s. Congress and its quickly assembled committees would have a field day. Who was to blame? Was Lockheed responsible for defective workmanship? Were the Navy and Coast Guard negligent in their support role and search efforts? Was there a clandestine White House role? Who knew? Was there a cover-up? And there were sinister implications. Earhart disappeared very close to Japanese held territories. Japan--a foreign power with whom diplomatic relations were becoming strained, one that had refused American entry to its mandated area. In the 1980s, the affair would be aired before the public in minute detail. Such an inquiry might have shed light on the true events; nevertheless, one was never launched. Curiously, no apparent effort at an investigation was made by government sources.

Faced with a dearth of post-disappearance information in official files, I concluded my leads must come from the turbulent news accounts of the event. A day did not pass, in the weeks and months following Amelia's disappearance, without some new, startling fact emerging. Amelia had been seen here, Fred Noonan there. They were alive and well. Letters were received from them under mysterious circumstances. The wreckage of the *Electra* had been spotted. No, they were dead. Yes, they were alive-- marooned on a remote Pacific Island. Notes in bottles washed up on shores from Australia to Long Beach.

Most appalling were the reports of radio messages, hundreds of them. An anxious public yearned for the safe return of its heroes, and most reports were sincere efforts to be helpful. Some, however, were cruel concoctions of sick minds. The reports followed official announcement of the missing airplane by only a few hours. Messages supposedly originating from the downed *Electra* placed it at various locations: afloat on the high seas northwest of Howland Island; crashed on an unknown reef; the beach of an atoll; intact but unable to take off again. Locations and circumstances seemed endless.

This was a time when mediums, in touch with the spirit world, were in vogue. They were urged by their ethereal contacts to direct search teams to particular locations (map provided at no extra cost). It seemed, as I waded through report after report, that false leads reached an all-time high during the search for Amelia Earhart.

But these leads were pursued, as best they could be; George Putnam saw to that. The official files I obtained included copies of numerous telegrams originating with Putnam. They were addressed to the White House, senior naval officers, ambassadors; the man's contacts seemed endless. When relayed to the Navy task force conducting the search, the messages followed a pattern: ...RELIABLE CONTACT REPORTS OBSERVING (HEARING) AN OBJECT, A VOICE, IN VICINITY OF SUCH AND SUCH. URGE SEARCH THIS SECTOR SOONEST... Putnam bore the cost of many of these diversions and one cannot be overly critical of the Navy for dutifully pursuing them. After all, only hindsight establishes the folly of disrupting precise standard operating procedures employed by an organization long experienced in conducting sea searches. Thinly veiled disgust with politically motivated interference can be read into reports submitted by the naval officers involved.

Its oversized internal fuel tank would permit the *Electra* to float indefinitely and a volunteer force of radio monitors immediately started receiving garbled messages to that effect. Unofficial sources explored and reported on the chances of Earhart and Noonan surviving a forced landing. They persisted, even after a spokesman for Lockheed stated the radio system installed in the *Electra* would function only on dry land.

Was there a lead buried in this mass of conflicting information? Admittedly uninformed on radio electronics, I started in search of authorities on radio broadcasting. My first question was usually, "Look, Earhart couldn't talk to that ship when she was almost on top of it. How can people from Maine to Australia claim to have heard her?"

Their usual reply, "There is a phenomenon connected to radio propagation called 'skip'. While many of the waves coming off a transmitting antenna travel along the surface, others are directed upward. At some point above the earth's surface they encounter a particle layer called the ionosphere. This layer reflects the wave back down toward the earth, at an angle. So, while signals paralleling the surface may fade after a couple of hundred miles, these skip signals can travel thousands, and still retain enough strength to be heard. They're freakish and totally unpredictable. In between the transmitter and where they are reflected back to the surface, you receive nothing, which is why they're called skip signals."

I didn't understand much of what I heard but I persisted. "I guess that accounts, then," I concluded, "for the fact that one man on the west coast sat up all night listening to Amelia trying to call ships and ground stations that couldn't receive her."

Usually a smile would accompany this reply. "Nothing is *impossible* in radio transmission but to receive a skip signal for that long approaches it. The ionosphere moves up and down, usually during hours of darkness. Many other disturbances can deflect the signal, like clouds and electrical storms. Conditions have to be just perfect; the area where the signal wave returns to the surface is quite small. You can sit here in one location and hear transmissions from all over, for a few, even several, minutes. But you may well never hear that station again."

"So you're telling me that virtually all of the people calling in these voices they heard were just plain liars?"

"Not necessarily. From the volume of reports, it appears that many people actually heard what they said they heard. More likely it was the transmission that was false, the work of some misguided ham radio operators hoping to create a sensation. Considering the state of the art in 1937, I would say the chances of anyone picking up a 'short-wave' broadcast (as it was then called) from Amelia's transmitter are remote, especially after any length of time. Even if she had been on dry land, without engine-driven generators, the batteries would not power her transmitter for more than a half hour or so. That equipment all had vacuum tubes, transformers and such that took a lot of amps, not like the solid state technology we use today."

Pondering this new information, I discarded any lead supposedly originating from the plane if it had ditched in open water. As I understood it, no water landing would leave an airplane "high and dry," like a boat. The electrical system would be the first casualty of water inside the fuselage.

Could they have crash landed on an island? A skeptical maybe, but reports showed that all islands within 500 miles of Earhart's destination had either been overflown or ground searched--*except* those islands inside Japanese territorial waters! I chafed under this yoke of research, wanting in the worst way to grab a shovel, head for the Pacific and start digging. But common sense told me not to make my move until I knew more about where and what I was searching.

I discovered that I really knew very little about Amelia Earhart as a person. Researching her life proved much easier, I discovered, than learning the truth about her fate. At least some hard facts existed here. I could still talk with people who remembered her. I visited with her sister, Muriel, and read biographical works. As I researched, my concept of this 39-year-old adventuress underwent a change. She was no publicity hungry stunt flyer; she was a warm, intelligent woman with great determination. Her childhood in the midwest was influenced by a stern grandfather--a judge with eastern blueblood lineage--and somewhat indulgent parents. From her mother's aristocratic side she learned the finer, ladylike, things of life and became an avid reader. She excelled at physics while in high school and loved to build things, create, use her hands.

Instinctive tomboy traits emerged at home. From the beginning she questioned the stereotyped roles of men and women, not in open rebellion or resentment, just with a sincere lack of understanding. Why were there no women locomotive engineers, for example? Amelia was a highly secure person, confident in her technical abilities. It puzzled her that more girls didn't share her feelings.

Always she was determined to control her own destiny, whether it be selection of schools, subjects to pursue or geographic location. When a particular school no longer interested her, she would move on. She went to Canada in 1917 to become a volunteer nurse, and during the flu epidemic the following year, contracted pneumonia. Loathing wasted time, she spent her protracted convalescence learning auto mechanics! Later she became an accomplished clothing designer. But always, she retained her charm. A childhood friend once said, "Amelia was always more fun to play with than other girls."

When she took up flying, it was with the same spirit of determination to succeed. She worked five days a week to earn the money for a flying lesson on Sunday. The air was her natural element; from her first flight she felt supremely secure. Flying became her release from mounting problems at home. Her father had become an alcoholic; her mother lost the last of her dwindling inheritance in a disastrous investment in a gypsum plant. Now on her own, Amelia vowed never to become dependent upon a man.

Her marriage then, to George Putnam, came as a surprise to many, including her mother. Putnam, thrice divorced, was known to be an impulsive, domineering type. The marriage was on Amelia's terms, however. Just prior to the ceremony she handed her husband-to-be her "declaration of independence." They would pursue their separate

careers, she told him. She would retain her maiden name
for publicity purposes. "...I cannot guarantee to endure at all
times the confinements of even an attractive cage." To the
surprise of many, the marriage flourished. Putnam became
her greatest supporter, relinquishing his duties with the
family publishing firm to promote her record-setting series
of flights.

Without doubt, Amelia was a pioneer feminist. She
accepted a lecture class at Purdue University to imbue
women with a feeling of self-confidence and independence.
She regarded her flying as a demonstration that women
could be competent in things requiring courage, skill and
dexterity.

It was said after her disappearance that Amelia was not
a good pilot. Critics cite problems Paul Mantz had with her
in training her to fly the big *Electra*, and her discarding of
essential equipment such as the trailing wire antenna and
the transmitter loading coil. But critics should consider the
attitude prevailing at the time Amelia learned to fly.
Sideslipping an airplane into a tiny cow pasture was a skill,
as was the ability to do a perfect "eight point" slow roll.
When trapped by bad weather, a pilot dropped beneath it
and followed roads, railroads, or power lines until a muddy
field could be found in which to land. The professionalism
we seek today in precision, planning and judgement was
just not used in evaluating flying skill in the 1920s and '30s.

I completed this phase of my research convinced that
whatever happened on that last flight was not due to
Earhart's inept flying technique. My admiration for the
woman had grown immeasurably.

Creation of a similar mental picture of Fred Noonan was
a different matter. Acquaintances' memories seemed more
vague and I noticed that previous Earhart historians
seemed to have encountered the same difficulty. Noonan
was highly visible, but he seemed to be faceless.

Gradually I discovered I was becoming more dedicated
to pursuing the mysterious disappearance of Amelia Earhart than the *Electra*. Until now, I had been attempting to
track Earhart as a means of getting a fix on that valuable

airplane. After all, Amelia and Noonan could not be brought back to life. On the other hand, the *Electra's* alloy metal could survive the elements, including the sea, indefinitely. When recovered, it could be seen and touched; its value was incalculable.

The civilized world has always had an aversion to consigning people to unmarked graves. The idea is unsettling; it arouses feelings of faint guilt and disrespect, not to give a loved one formal last rites. Common decency demanded that someone stand over this courageous woman's place of final rest and give proper tribute.

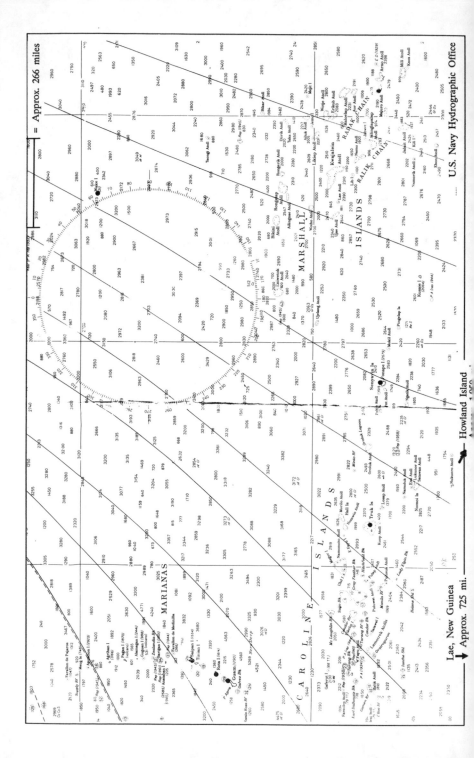

Lae, New Guinea
Approx. 725 mi.

Howland Island

= Approx. 266 miles

U.S. Navy Hydrographic Office

Chapter Five:
THE SPY THEORY

Now I plunged headlong into the real rat's nest of conjecture, rumor and contradiction. It was time to narrow down the list of possible sites where that controversial flight of July third* had terminated. I decided first to tackle the notion that Amelia Earhart was on a spying mission in the western Pacific. To accept this theory could change Amelia's probable point of disappearance by several hundred miles. Simply stated, the spy theory contends that Amelia was recruited by individuals or an agency in the U.S. government to overfly territory under Japanese mandate. She would observe, taking pictures if possible, any signs of fortification in progress. This information obviously would be invaluable to President Roosevelt and other military leaders.

The territory that includes the Marshall and Mariana Islands had been mandated to Japan after World War I, but a portion of that mandate stipulated that the territory would not be used for military purposes. Informal reports indicated that Japan was creating offensive military capabilities in violation of its mandate. The leaders of nations in southeast Asia and Australia were convinced that Japan was on the verge of launching a military campaign.

FDR and a handful of his most loyal, trusted aids were facing a growing militancy abroad. Hard information regard-

---

* The flight originated in Lae, New Guinea on July 3. As the Electra crossed the International Date Line the calendar reverted one day; thus the landing occurred on July 2.

ing intent was almost impossible to obtain. First, the armed forces were on extremely austere budgets. The generals and admirals were more concerned with keeping their guns and ships operational than gathering intelligence, and their attitude toward a potential attack was one of complacency, almost arrogance. What nation would dare cross almost 2,000 miles of ocean to attack the mighty United States?

Second, FDR's cabinet and the Congress were occupied with domestic problems, mostly financial. Intelligence was not in their purview; that was a job for the military. The prevailing attitude toward clandestine or covert operations was a chivalrous "Gentlemen do not read other people's mail." To the public, ignorance was bliss. Hitler and Tojo were names in the news, but nothing to take too seriously.

That FDR had a basis for suspicion is borne out in official histories of the Pacific war. Japan deployed warships and aircraft in the area on a permanent basis long before 1941. That ground defenses would accompany this deployment is a logical conclusion. But official histories indicate that an intensive effort to construct land based fortifications in the Marshalls and Marianas was *not* made prior to 1941. Ironically Japan's refusal to permit our search craft into that area was very likely an effort to conceal the *absence* of strong defenses.

The President had other information that was provided to Admiral Tarnell on Honolulu by a French civilian named de Bisshop. The latter reported that when he visited the island of Jaluit (Marshall Islands) in 1937 he saw shells for three-inch guns being unloaded but not the guns themselves...The Japanese had dragged and dredged the harbor until it was much larger and freer from obstruction than shown on current charts...A concrete airplane ramp... hangars and shops...Upon learning that de Bisshop had sailed close to Mili atoll, the Japanese became very angry. He was told that work going on there was so secret that even Japanese merchant ships were not allowed near the tiny island. This information was obviously enough to give Roosevelt cause for concern. In that political climate, FDR may well have viewed Amelia's flight, which bordered

Japanese territory, as a clever way to learn what might be going on out there. A simple navigational error a few degrees off course, who could dispute it?

Additionally, a strong personal tie existed between Amelia and the White House. Eleanor Roosevelt was captivated by this young woman, petite in appearance but aggressive in nature. Amelia was a frequent visitor and recipient of warm messages of congratulations for her exploits from both the President and his wife. One of FDR's "Fireside Chats" with Amelia mentions an opportunity for her to render invaluable service to her country... Amelia possessed a somewhat quixotic streak and might well have found vicarious appeal in the idea. While her around-the-world venture was in preparation, she had reportedly said to her mother, "There are things I can't tell you about this flight."

Another scenario involved Earhart's husband, George Putnam, who by this time had discovered that his wife's heroic flights were often not financially rewarding. For her round-the-world flight he concocted a scheme with Gimble's Department Store in New York to sell envelopes pre-addressed to the buyer. Amelia would post them from stops along her route. The idea was only mildly successful, producing far less revenue than that required for financing the trip. Considering Putnam's sometimes Machiavellian approach to business and his own access to the White House, it would not be out of character for him to suggest casually that Amelia could gather some valuable intelligence if the government would provide financial assistance for the trip. Certainly FDR was not above taking a personal hand in clandestine matters of state; he rather enjoyed it. Putnam was, in fact, visited at his operating base at the Oakland Airfield by uniformed personnel and high level emissaries such as Gene Vidal of the Department of Commerce and Richard Black from the Department of the Interior.

That the Navy would initiate such a scheme is doubtful. First, not many of the top brass saw any urgency in determining Japan's military designs. Second, professional

intelligence gathering agencies have a pronounced aversion
to working with amateurs. Amelia was known to be
impulsive and often unpredictable. Noonan had a long
history of alcoholism. Putnam was deeply involved in public
relations, a profession incompatible with high level secret
operations.

In the classification hierarchy pertaining to government
documents, OFFICIAL USE ONLY, RESTRICTED and
CONFIDENTIAL identify material which would be inimical
to public interest. SECRET and TOP SECRET are used
when documents contain information that could be highly
damaging to national security. Some military bases with
sensitive missions classify their internal telephone direc-
tories CONFIDENTIAL. Any plan having to do with
gathering intelligence would be given a classification of at
least SECRET, more likely TOP SECRET. Yet the highest
classification ever assigned to any Earhart-related docu-
ment provided me was CONFIDENTIAL. The solemn announcement that access had been granted to previously
SECRET files was largely a bunch of fluff!

This revelation could be highly significant. Assume the
Navy Department had acted under pressure from FDR.
Senior military officers have a penchant for making a
"memo for record" when they foresee a backlash from
carrying out a directive from a higher headquarters. These
are known as CYA actions, an acronym for Cover Your A__.
Undoubtedly such memos were written if White House
coercion were applied. Admiral Chester Nimitz reportedly
said prior to his death, "When the American public learns
the true story about Amelia Earhart, they won't believe it."*

The Freedom of Information Act can produce a wealth
of formerly safeguarded information, but the request must
be quite specific--a precaution to prevent writers and
researchers from going on "fishing trips" in the hope that a
story will emerge. Personally, I think we've been asking for
the wrong files. The files made available to me *do* show a
level of government support for Amelia's flight in excess of

---

* From Fred Goerner's *The Search for Amelia Earhart*

that afforded any similar project by private interests.
Example: Amelia requested air to air refueling in Mid-
Pacific. A Navy feasibility study showed it was possible and
the idea was approved in principle. Later, it was determined
that an airstrip on tiny Howland Island would better serve
as a refueling stop. Howland, then under authority of the
Department of Commerce (DOC), was promptly transferred
to the Department of Interior (DOI). Why? Perhaps because
DOC had no funds to build an airstrip, while DOI had
money appropriated under the Public Works Act.

Additional assistance came from the Coast Guard which
ordered the cutter *Itasca* to stand off Howland Island to
provide radio navigation assistance. The USS tug *Ontario*
and USS *Swan* were positioned along the proposed flight
path.

My files contain the copy of a memo on Navy Department letterhead dated November 1936 to the Chief of
Naval Operations. It is signed /Paul Bastedo/ and reads as
follows:

THE ATTACHED LETTER WAS HANDED ME
THIS MORNING, TOGETHER WITH THE
INFORMATION THAT THE PRESIDENT
HOPED THE NAVY WOULD DO WHAT THEY
COULD TO COOPERATE WITH MISS AMELIA
EARHART IN HER PROPOSED FLIGHT AND
THAT IN THIS CONNECTION, CONTACT
SHOULD BE MADE WITH HER HUSBAND, MR.
PUTNAM.

It would appear that Amelia's flight had White House
support, but why? Friendship or official interest? In view of
federal budget crunches FDR faced at the time, a personal
tie would have to have been extremely close. As it was, he
drew strong criticism for his assistance, especially for the
cost of the search effort. If Amelia agreed with the
President to do what she could on an informal verbal basis,
a lack of documentation is not surprising. FDR would have
taken care that his critics in Congress and the staunch
isolationists in his cabinet remained uninformed about his

agreement. It is unlikely that senior military officers would require a detailed reason for extensive support. Questioning orders originating from the White House can be hazardous to promotion.

There are two troubling contradictions to the spy theory. One, Earhart's flight plan from Lae, New Guinea to Howland would place her in the vicinity of key Japanese installations after the hours of darkness--not the best of times for making an aerial survey. Two, not one shred of hard evidence has ever been produced from official files to support the theory. Historically, people in high places become compulsive talkers after leaving their government posts, consumed by an urge to share their exclusive story. Of course these disclosures are usually quite lucrative. However, not one such person has come forward with information on the spy theory in almost 50 years.

Any conclusion based on the *absence* of evidence is usually weak. In actuality, Earhart could have been over the Caroline Islands before full dark (Truk was a major Japanese stronghold) or the Marshall Islands just at daybreak. Theoretically the plane was fueled for a range of 4,000 miles; the distance to Howland was 2,555 miles.*

The spy theory was an important factor in locating a probable crash site. If it were true, I could almost abandon any search south of her planned course. If it were not, I was back to the search records and the ham radio operators' questionable reports of transmissions after the crash.

It was tempting to accept the conclusions of Goerner, Loomis, and others that she had gone down in Japanese territory, but I had vowed from the beginning not to let myself be influenced by anything other than official accounts. Still, I knew it could be detrimental to ignore *all* previous research. Perhaps my predecessors had uncovered information after their books were published that could help me; with the exception of Loomis, their works were 15 to 20 years old.

---

* The reader may notice an apparent discrepancy in milages when reading different accounts. Nautical navigators use the nautical mile which equals 1.15 statute or land miles; over land pilots commonly use the statute mile.)

The only encouraging news I obtained from other researchers was from Joe Gervais. He believes that a heretofore unread classified file may exist and promised to contact me if he were successful in obtaining it.

In the midst of my frustration over a lack of substantial, documented evidence on the Earhart case, my son Tom, a lawyer, offered some valuable insights. "Maybe you're expecting too much," Tom suggested. If so-called 'hard' evidence existed, the thing would have been solved and forgotten long before now. If you were submitting this to a jury we would say you had to build your case on circumstantial evidence. There's nothing wrong with that. A lot of settlements and convictions are based on it. Sometimes direct testimony just isn't possible. You rely on the Reasonable Man principle."

"Reasonable Man?"

"The Reasonable Man is a person of average intelligence and totally without bias or prejudice. You always hope you have twelve of them on a jury."

"I'd like to find just *one* of these 'Reasonable Men,'" I thought to myself grimly.

"For instance," Tom continued, "Farmer Jones has a flock of sheep. Farmer Brown has a dog, well-known and easily recognized in the area. Neighbors see this dog chasing Jones' sheep on several occasions. One day Jones comes home and finds several of his sheep slaughtered, apparently killed by an animal. He goes to Brown's house; the dog is there. It has wool in its teeth and blood all over its muzzle. Now Reasonable Man will conclude that Brown's dog killed the sheep, even though no one actually saw it happen.

"So *you* become 'Reasonable Man.' In the absence of direct testimony *you* draw conclusions from related, believable, information."

Tom's words made sense. It was foolish to think I would find signed affidavits, pictures, etc. in profusion. If even half the reports of Earhart's having been sighted as a captive of the Japanese Army could be believed, the *Japanese* at least were convinced that Earhart was on a spying mission.

Reasonable Man would conclude that at least there had been a plan and an attempt for Earhart to make an intelligence gathering diversion.

I felt better. I had now narrowed my initial search area to a mere 10,000 square miles of ocean.

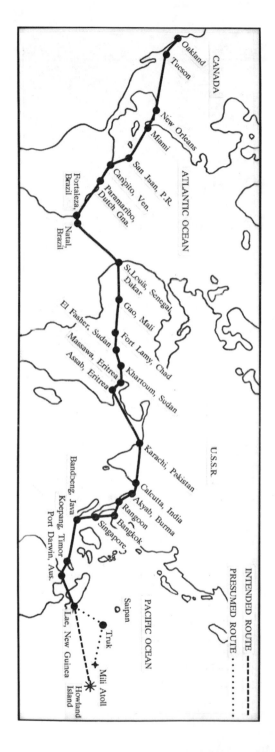

Route of Amelia's Last Flight

Chapter Six:
THE FLIGHT

I conceded, reluctantly, that reducing the search area for Amelia's crash site involved reconstructing her flight path. It was a distasteful prospect. A large wall map of the South Pacific had been one of my first acquisitions. I was soon proficient at latitudes and longitudes and had covered the map with little x's, circles, lines, different colors, etc. It looked very impressive--and I couldn't make heads nor tails of it.

The longer I worked, the clearer it became that Earhart's flight path, real or imagined, had nothing to do with my project. She had gone down regardless of how she managed to miss Howland Island. I put the map out of my mind.

One version of Earhart's disappearance had the *Electra* crashing on the island of Saipan, about 1,500 hundred miles from her destination--as far off course as she could get without flying a reverse course. The Navy had her down in open water north of Howland. Another version had her crashing in the Marshall Islands. Then there were those radio voices after the crash; they had plotted like a shotgun pattern on researchers' maps. Finally there was the version that had her deliberately landing on a Japanese held island and smuggled back to the United States. It was time to formulate my version and I needed help.

Vaguely I recalled that my friend Ray Rosenbaum had flown B-17 bombers during World War II, which would have put him in flight training not too long after Amelia went down. I also remembered that just before his retirement he had flown C-130's on supply missions to Southeast Asia during the Vietnam War. He would have flown several trips very close to the route Amelia had followed. I tracked him down.

After I told him my intentions and my discoveries, he shook his head. "Buddy, you're talking about searching a place that's nothing but miles and miles of nothing but miles and miles. This thing happened more than 40 years ago! People that could tell you anything aren't just standing around on street corners. Don't you think that the others who have tried to find her have milked witnesses and records of what little information may have existed?" I was getting a little tired of hearing these arguments. Finally, he surrendered. "Okay, okay, I'll take a look."

Ensconced in my little private office, surrounded by cartons containing my research efforts and numerous books on Earhart's disappearance, Ray examined the material covering NR 16020's last flight. It was dark when I returned to pick him up for dinner, and he barely acknowledged my presence as I let myself in. He was standing in front of my wall map, a pair of dividers in hand, a scowl of concentration on his face. The precious documentation I had spent hours cataloguing and filing lay strewn over half the room. Finally he tossed the dividers on the desk and glared at me. "Buddy, this is the biggest, most garbled, mess I've ever seen! Half this stuff doesn't make sense and what does is contradicted a half dozen times." Over dinner, he went to great lengths to explain what was wrong with everything he had read that afternoon. I listened patiently. I could afford to--I had old Ray hooked!

We returned to the office. Ray slumped to the sofa and propped his feet on a coffee table. "All right," he said, "You want to know where I think she came down? From what I've seen, she could have come down almost anyplace."

He chuckled at my disgusted look. "Seriously, there is a lot of room for error. I know what you're faced with though and I'll do my best to help eliminate some of the possibilities. "If I were to start putting chips on the table," he said, tapping several sheets of microfilm copy, "I would put a big stack on this thing."

I leaned forward to look. The top sheet read REPORT OF EARHART SEARCH - LEXINGTON GROUP - U. S. S. LEXINGTON - FLAGSHIP JULY 1937. *(See Appendix A)*

"This represents the efforts of five ships and about 40 airplanes over a two week period. These were professionals at conducting sea searches, not reporters motivated to turn up something sensational for a newspaper, magazine or radio contract. A massive search effort--the most extensive to that date. You have to question why they didn't find anything. That *Electra* was carrying 75 gallons of engine oil when it left Lae Field. Some would have been used during flight, of course, but if that airplane went down at sea, the remainder would have seeped out. Do you have any idea how big an oil slick 50 gallons of engine oil makes and how long it remains? It isn't like gasoline; it doesn't evaporate.

"If the plane had broken apart on impact, there were all sorts of things inside that would have floated. *Some* of them eventually would have washed up on a beach. It leads you to believe there wasn't anything to find in the area they searched, yet it was the most logical place to search."

"I've read a lot of reports like this," Ray went on. "This one is well written, by experts. But many people make a mistake when they start looking for what went wrong. They look first at the assumptions and conclusions, but the subject to question is the facts. What if the *facts* are in error?

"Let's look at 'known fact' number 15. The plane's position at 0720 GCT (Greenwich Civil Time)...this was the only complete position report received. What makes that a fact? Because that's where Earhart *said* she was. There was no radar in those days, so nobody saw her. At Nauru Island she was expected to pass overhead. Again, she talked by radio, said she saw lights, (later than her flight plan called for) but the people outside looking and listening for the airplane didn't see or hear a thing.

"Was she faking it? That is, was she already lost so she made a position report based on dead reckoning where she *should* have been? I've done this, I must confess. You're blundering along there in the soup and it's time for your routine position report. You give them your flight plan position even though you could well be 50 miles from that spot. But in this case, she was flying in clear weather, during daylight, and following this little chain of islands, the Solomons. One of them, Nukumanu, was one of Earhart's preplanned checkpoints.

"Now Buddy, I'm far from being fully convinced of the spy theory," Ray went on. But if she filed one flight plan intending actually to fly a totally different one, she wasn't over Nukumanu at 0720 GCT, which blows the Navy search logic completely out of the water! I mention this because it can help us later in calculating where she ran out of fuel. If she was indeed at Nukumanu at that time, flying her filed flight plan, she was in trouble already and had to know it. She was almost an hour behind flight plan and only a third of the way to her destination. There was no hope of making up that time from the forecast she received. Now granted, the weather she actually encountered bore little resemblance to the forecast. The flight center at Honolulu was most candid when it announced: 'Accurate forecast difficult because of lack of reports.' A weather forecast *must* be based on observation, especially winds aloft, if you're flying. There *were* no reporting stations out there at the time, because the Japs controlled everything to the north.

"An airplane is a free floating object. It moves with the wind in exact proportion to the wind's speed and direction. If you're flying east, say, at 150 M.P.H. and the wind blows from the north at 30, you're going to move south at 30 miles an hour at the same time you are going east at 150. There's no way you can know that unless you take 'fixes' of your position on the surface. A winds aloft forecast is most essential.

"Earhart had strong headwinds and the few reports available are consistent in wind direction--from the east northeast. The *Ontario* was reporting winds of 'force three'. That's navy talk for about 20 M.P.H. on the surface. Wind velocity increases with altitude. Notice Howland's winds

aloft report, from 14 M.P.H. on the surface to 31 at 8,000
feet. Personally, I don't think they ever got as far east as
Howland. The *Lexington* report comes to that conclusion
too.

"The report also concludes that something, a leak or
poor carburetor mixture control, diminished their fuel
supply. I think I can tell you what happened to that extra
gas. They used it trying to get on top so Noonan could get a
celestial fix. He must have been desperate for a position fix
after running for several hours on dead reckoning. To do
this, you set climb power, which requires a rich mixture,
and hang by the props until you get as high as you can go,
way above your most efficient cruising altitude. If you don't
break out, you're going to encounter icing conditions in
those clouds, so you come back down. Pretty soon you try it
again. Believe me, this uses gas. It's probably the way
Noonan got that sun line. You can do a reasonable sun shot
through thin clouds sometimes.

"One last point. Howland and the *Itasca* were in clear
weather but reporting a heavy cloud bank to the north and
west. Amelia reported being 'in clouds' and 'under an
overcast'. By my calculations, they would have ended up
short and to the north of course."

I considered his words and pondered some of the
reports. "How about those radio signals received on board
Itasca? They were very strong. *Itasca* thought she was
within less than 50 miles."

"She might have been, but radio propagation, especially
in the frequencies she was using, is at its most freakish
around dawn and dusk. She could have been 200 miles
away, or more. She wasn't reading *Itasca* was she? But even
that doesn't mean much. Flying in visible moisture with
those old sets, you might as well turn off your receiver, for
you'll get nothing but static."

"Ray, are you telling me you think she went down in the
Marshalls? The Navy search didn't turn up a clue; the
Japanese wouldn't let us search their territory."

"Low and outside is my best deduction. Now a man
named Rafford who reconstructed the probable flight path

for Vincent Loomis made some shrewd deductions and might even be right. But Buddy, any attempt to retrace that flight with such surgical precision is a waste of time. First, we don't know for sure that Amelia ever intended to follow her flight plan as filed. It's possible that when she encountered unexpected weather and was running ahead of her fuel consumption curve, she decided to abort the spy mission and head straight for Howland from some unknown point up north. Second, no one then or now knew what the weather *really* was like that night, especially the winds. 'Severe squalls' were forecast and no pilot likes to head straight through those if he can see a way around them. They usually run 30 to 50 miles in diameter. So you circumnavigate north of one, south of another, always trying to return to your original course line but you can't be sure. You can fly over half the Pacific dodging those rain storms.

"I won't speculate as far as to pinpoint a landing site. For one thing the only firm time established is when radio contact was lost. She could have flown for an hour, even two after that. She reported, I believe, 'running low on fuel--30 minutes remaining'. The fuel gauges we used then were not all that accurate, especially near full and near empty. You always see the worst when you're around empty. With the power pulled back and the mixture leaned out next to starvation, she wouldn't have burned more than 30 or 35 gallons per hour. I won't speculate any further, but I can tell you something of what it would have been like to sit in the cockpit of NR16020 that night."

I had had enough flying lessons for one evening, but Ray ignored me and continued. "Have you ever considered strapping yourself in the front seat of your car and setting out to drive nonstop for 20 hours?"

I couldn't help adding, "I guess you're going to give the road map to a drunk and put him behind a plywood partition in the back seat."

"You're referring to the stories about Noonan being on an all night party before takeoff? I wouldn't put too much stock in that. Noonan was a pro. He would have been in shape to fly. There *were* two versions of that, remember. Drunk or sober, he *did* do some navigating, some pretty good navigating to get them as close as he did. But let's ignore Noonan for now.

You're in the left seat. Takeoff is hairy. The *Electra* is grossly overweight and you're forced to use the lift afforded by ground effect to gain airspeed, just skimming the surface of the water. You glue your eyes on that rate of climb indicator; up, up, please go up! A quick glance at the airspeed indicator. You're bordering on stall speed. You're approaching the time limit you can keep those engines at full takeoff power. Finally 100 feet per minute, 200; you're gaining altitude! A slight gain in airspeed; you ease a fraction of power off the straining engines. What if you lost an engine at this point? Even if you *could* nurse the thing back to the field, you'd blow a tire landing with this weight. You're very conscious of that big tank of av-gas sitting at your right elbow.

You pass through 1,000 feet. You're at normal climb power, not gaining altitude very rapidly but things settle down. You notice it's hot inside the cockpit, you're drenched. You slide your side window back slightly to get some air. For the first time you notice fumes from the internal fuel tank.

Noonan passes a new heading to you on the end of the fishing rod stowed over the fuel tank. You make the slight correction of heading and set up the autopilot, a Godsend, that autopilot. You glance at the empty right seat. Secretly you would prefer a person over there instead of the auto pilot, but this is *your* big trip; no other human to lean on. The plane wants to enter a slight turn to the left. You adjust the fine tuning knobs on the auto pilot. It flies straight but now it wants to wallow, a corkscrewing motion like a boat. After more adjustments it finally settles down.

You're at 8,000 feet now. Noonan passes you a message to level out, which means you go through the whole auto pilot adjustment routine again. Looking around you notice little flecks of pretty vegetation dot the water's surface. You consult the topographical map you drew up yourself. Noonan uses a different variety. Although your map shows mostly vast expanses of blue it's a kind familiar to you. A red grease pencil line with little cross bars every hundred miles marks your course.

You look at the airspeed; quite a bit lower than usual-- almost 10 M.P.H. slower. It will pick up, you reason, as you burn off some of that fuel. Momentarily flustered, you realize you were supposed to have read the fuel tanks on the hour and have forgotten. You study the gauges and guess what they would have read.

Noonan passes you a position report. You pick up the microphone, check to see that everything is properly tuned, and call Lae. The prompt, cheery "receiving you loud and clear, go ahead" is reassuring. You read off the position report and close down, then try to plot on your map the latitude and longitude Noonan has given you. This can't be right. The big land mass off the left wing has to be New Britain; it checks with your map. You've covered only a little more than a hundred miles! You dig through the briefcase to find that weather forecast. Winds for the first leg, east southeast at 12-15--it must be closer to 30! The course correction was to the left, (north) and the wind is supposed to be from the south quadrant. You scribble a note to Noonan, "Shall we go to a lower altitude for better wind?" The curt 'no' leaves you faintly displeased and you opt for lunch.

A look at the clock shows it's almost time for another position report. You look forward to hearing that cheerful voice at the other end, but it's finished all too soon. A whole hour to wait now until the next one. You scan the radio frequencies hoping to hear a friendly voice, but get only one garbled conversation in a foreign language and some blurred Morse code.

Time drags. You're bored. You sing to yourself. The engines drone on. You adjust the prop controls to keep them in exact synchronization, otherwise they set up a rhythm that grates on the nerves. The autopilot gives off little noises as it makes the control movements to keep you on course. It is slaved to a gyroscopic compass that is supposed to hold a steady heading but seems to be precessing to the left. The manual says to reset the gyro compass to the magnetic compass every 10 or 15 minutes, but you're doing this about every five minutes just to keep occupied.

The big island of Bougainville comes and goes. The brief glimpse of people below is cheering; a long stretch of open water lies before the next landfall. A look at your map shows you are still losing time against your flight plan, but the overloaded fuel tank should give you ample reserve.

An extremely distasteful problem develops--a warning signal from your bladder but there is no room to leave your seat. A hard rubber funnel underneath the seat is connected to a flexible tube which passes through the floor of the airplane to the outside. The people at Burbank had done their best to redesign the rig for a female pilot, but it is still a most unsatisfactory arrangement. At last the ordeal is over but the fact that it will have to be done again before the night is over is depressing.

The island of Nukumanu finally drifts into view, but maybe 20 miles to your left. If it had been a bit more to the right, you would have missed it! You're almost an hour behind schedule. The sun is well down now and the little island makes a picturesque setting in the low angle of sunlight. Further east however, the scene is less enrapturing. A sullen line of clouds mar the horizon. The fluffy cumulus that have been beneath you for the past hour begin to thicken. Shortly after passing Nukumanu you are flying over solid undercast. In a matter of minutes, it seems, the sun also disappears behind clouds. Now you can see ominous flickers of lightning in the clouds ahead. You pass your position report to Lae, still loud and clear, which is reassuring. Suddenly it is dark. You adjust the ultraviolet instrument lamps to their lowest setting so as to retain your night vision.

Noonan can see nothing ahead from his little cell in the back, so you advise him of the change in weather and tell him you'll attempt to circumnavigate the biggest clouds. Instinct tells you to go down to just above water level and try to stay beneath the clouds, but it's been six hours since you had an altimeter pressure setting--too risky.

You strain your eyes looking for a 'soft spot.' There aren't many. You dodge a couple then blunder right into a granddaddy which causes the airplane to buck like a mad bull. No autopilot now for its gyro tumbles out of control with about thirty degrees of bank. Rain lashes the windshield, eliminating all hope of seeing a light spot. You struggle to keep the *Electra* upright. From the corner of your eye you see a message on the end of the fishing pole. While trying to fly with the left hand, you attempt to read the communique in the dim glow of the instrument lights. Frustrated, you throw the message to the floor and concentrate on flying. After a brief respite you find a flashlight and retrieve the message. It's your position report. You attempt to call Lae, but there's no response. The *Ontario* should be within range, but the earphones are so full of static that you can't be sure if there was an acknowledgement or not. You give your position 'in the blind' which is all you have time for before you're back in the heavy clouds again.

The night drags on. Noonan is passing up messages like snowflakes. "Can you get a radio fix? Any possibility of getting on top for a star shot? What's the fuel reading? My compass shows us seven degrees off course, what does your's read?" The messages become more urgent. "MUST get a celestial fix or radio fix." What does he expect you to do about it? You squirm around, trying to find a more comfortable position. Noonan's right about the compass heading. You've been flying by the gyro; the magnetic compass is free floating. It swings so erratically in this rough weather, however, that you can only average out its readings. Irritated, you discover you've forgotten to reset the gyro; you do your best to get an approximate reset.

The fuel reading announces itself in a most emphatic manner--nothing attracts attention like a red light on an airplane instrument panel! Like a huge evil eye the red

light over the right-hand fuel gauge casts a rosy glow over
the darkened cockpit. You swallow your heart; you were
supposed to have transferred fuel from the internal tank
more than an hour ago! You grasp the handle of the
'wobble' pump and work furiously. After what seems like
ages the offending light winks off. As you continue pumping
you wonder, "Isn't it too early for that main tank to run
dry?" You'd like to check but you're flying with one hand,
pumping with the other. It's too much to get the flashlight
and find the fuel log; that will have to wait.

Abruptly the jolting, lurching turbulence ceases. You
look into the clear night and see stars through towering
cloud columns. You scramble for notepaper; Noonan will get
his chance. Halfway through the note, however, you've
reentered clouds. "I'll turn around, find the hole again and
spiral up, again," you decide. You wrench the wheel over
and reverse course. Five minutes pass. Nothing. You must
have missed it to the south. Another turn; you've lost it.
For the first time tears of frustration burn your eyes.
Another note from Noonan, "What are you doing? Is
something wrong?" You feel like taking that fishing pole,
breaking it into nine pieces and throwing it out the window!
You resume pumping. The main tank gauges barely edge to
the right.

If that one hole existed, there must be others, you
reason. Maybe you're flying out of the storm system. It
can't hurt to go up and take a look. You pass your
intentions to Noonan and set climb power, struggling
through 10,000 feet, then 11,000. More turbulence as you
near the cloud tops at 12,000. The rate of climb is next to
nothing as you pass 13,000. Nearing 14,000 there is no
indication of breaking out and you've just about reached
your ceiling. You switch on a landing light; maybe the
clouds are thinning. It's like looking into a bucket of milk.

Suddenly you're electrified by the rattle of something
sounding like handfuls of gravel striking the sides of the
airplane. Prop ice! It's being slung off by the centrifugal
force of the spinning props. A flashlight beam along the
leading edge of the wing confirms your diagnosis. A white

line of what looks to be innocent frost is visible, but you know it isn't innocent. Reduce power, lower the nose. Get back down below the freezing level. No star shot this time. You just have to break out of this stuff!

The ride is smoothing. Pressing your face against the window, you can make out the tops of clouds only a few feet beneath you in the dim illumination of the wing navigation light. Above all is darkness, however. You're between layers but at least you can risk setting up the auto pilot again. You want to check your map and the fuel log. You haven't made an entry for two or three hours, but you must stay on that wobble pump. Your arm feels as if it will drop off. Disgusted with fumbling around in the dark, with only a puny flashlight, you snap on the overhead cockpit lights. To hell with precious night vision! There's nothing to see out there but clouds anyway.

You sink back in the seat and let fatigue wash over you in great waves. Looking at the clock, you have difficulty remembering your takeoff time. Finally you calculate it has been almost 13 hours. You'll rest a bit then get back to pumping fuel. All the bouncing in those clouds has caused fumes from the internal tank to become more noticeable, and you can feel a headache coming.

You're startled and confused by a substantial jolt through your seat. Where are you? Everything comes back with a rush. Good God you've fallen asleep! The airplane is running in and out of cloud tops, giving you a bump each time. You clear your eyes and look at the clock, but can't remember when you checked it. Try to make radio contact again. The *Itasca* has powerful equipment; maybe it's in range now. No answer on any frequency. The cockpit is a mess. The lunch box has bounced off the right seat and its contents litter the floor. The fuel log is hopelessly behind. You transfer the remainder of the fuel to main tanks and try to calculate in hours how much is left. Sweeping the controls, your eyes widen in horror as you look closely at the fuel mixture control levers in the rich position! You moved them to rich for the climb and forgot to lean out the mixture again! Close to panic you make a hurried adjustment, a futile effort to make amends for your error.

You fight exhaustion. The outside world is definitely growing lighter. You can see water through breaks in the clouds beneath you, but a solid overcast persists. A note from Noonan. "See if you can get high enough for me to get a sun line." You begrudge the extra fuel the climb will cost but set the power and try again.

Success! At 12,000 the sun is visible as a pale yellow disk through the haze. You hold the plane as steady as possible while Noonan uses his sextant. He completes his calculations and passes up what will be the best position estimate you will have. To your surprise he places you within 200 miles of Howland. Back to the radio. It seems that at times you are getting a response so you keep trying.

The urge to get down where you can see is overpowering. You lower the nose and break out below the cloud base at well over a thousand feet. You scan the horizon but the view is barren; gray water in all directions. Your eyes burn with fatigue, body tissues are dehydrated by altitude and your mouth is dry and foul tasting. To your left an island seems to appear. You head in that direction, but the image disappears. A curt note from Noonan advises to stay on course. You have trouble remembering what the original heading was.

You curse the obstructing right seat; if only you could see better over there. Straight ahead and to your left is your entire entire field of vision. You are so tired; more futile calls on the radio. For the first time you let yourself ask that all pervasive question, "Are we going to make it?"

Ray leaned back, drained by his bizarre account. I had sat transfixed by what he was telling me. I managed to ask in little more than a whisper "My God, could it have been that bad?"

"Every bit, Buddy. At one time or another I have gone through everything I described to you. The Monday morning quarterbacks can tell you in great detail everything she did wrong, but fatigue breeds mistakes. An old slogan on the walls of half the flight operations rooms in the country goes something like this, 'Aviation, in itself, is not inherently dangerous. But like the sea, it is terribly unforgiving of mistakes.' Earhart and Noonan exceeded their limitations and paid the price."

And, I thought to myself, if I'm right they spotted a little shallow lagoon behind a reef or a strip of sandy beach. In spite of her condition, Amelia made a near perfect landing and stepped right into the waiting arms of the Japanese Army!

Mike Harris   **T.C. Brennan III**

**Film Crew: from left, Ben Berry, Buddy
Brennan, Mike Harris, NIK**

Chapter Seven:
THE SEARCH

Actually there were two searches conducted for the downed aircraft. The first was an impressive Coast Guard and Navy effort. The second was without government participation and delayed by an intervening war which changed the entire complexion of territorial holdings in the Pacific. The first search lasted 18 days. The second one, launched more than 20 years later, continues to this day. A consensus may never be reached as to what transpired in the crucial six months between March and August, 1937. The searchers that preceded me are themselves far from agreement.

To fully appreciate the extent of the Navy search, please refer to Appendices A and B. Six vessels steamed 48,000 miles to search 94,800 square miles. Naval aircraft logged 1,654 hours covering 167,481 square miles. This effort is akin to searching the state of Texas which has an area of 267,000 square miles.

Two aspects of this search interested me. One was the enormous amount of time and manpower devoted to it. At a time when a million dollars would nearly *buy* a naval vessel, the U.S. spent as much as *four million*--and in the face of an angry outcry from the public at such an expenditure! FDR faced some stormy press conferences and an angry public over the matter. Does this imply that the flight had a purpose other than just setting a world record?

The second aspect that intrigued me was the Japanese reaction. Japanese documents obtained after the war show that they suspected the U.S. would use the search to make intelligence gathering overflights. While the official report submitted by the *Lexington* group is most complete, one portion is suspect. The reported search area is confined to American waters. Presumably the pilots searched where they *said* they searched, but no one was there to monitor them. It would be naive to think that one or two were not diverted quickly to the Marshalls, a scant hundred miles away. Is this a possible reason for the magnitude of the Navy search?

Official files indicate that a formal request through diplomatic channels for permission to search inside Japanese mandated waters was politely refused. The Japanese countered with assurance that their vessels would conduct a thorough search. They were most generous with details, stating that ships of their Squadron 12, with assistance from the *Koshu* and *Kamoi*, would participate.

The Japanese continued to provide reports of negative results well into September, and quite understandably--documents obtained after World War II place Squadron 12 and the *Kamoi* in their home ports during a time when they were supposed to be searching the Marshall Islands area some 2,000 miles distant! The log of the *Koshu* revealed no hint that it was conducting a search.

The Japanese were meticulous record keepers. Failure to destroy incriminating documents led to the downfall of many during the War Crimes Trials. Yet no record was ever uncovered establishing official knowledge of Amelia Earhart being apprehended. *Every* bit of information points to the plane crashing in the Marshalls; *none* exists to refute it. Yet the two countries involved have not the slightest shred of official confirmation.

How could such documents simply vanish? Highly classified files are not casually expunged. If the subject received high level attention, evidence always exists in multiple locations--in our military archives as well as Japan's. The war is long over; how could release of these documents still "prove damaging to national security?" I encounter this conundrum repeatedly--there is no confirmation of reported events where there *should* be confirmation; or if the report is incorrect, there is no evidence to establish it *is* incorrect. Just when you get excited over a solid lead and turn to the official record for verification, you encounter a void.

I see two explanations for missing records. One asks us to believe that more than two dozen people who claim to have seen Earhart, Noonan and/or the airplane in Japanese custody are lying or were totally mistaken. Ergo, there is no reason why official documentation would have been created. There were no clandestine aspects to the flight. The Japanese searched the area and found nothing because the aircraft went down at sea and sank immediately. As Dick Strippel rationalizes in his book *Amelia Earhart: The Myth and the Reality*, "If there is, or was, such a (intelligence gathering) plot, its blood-sworn to secrecy participants range from Navy and Coast Guard seamen through admirals; from newspaper stringers through Cabinet secretaries in the administrations of four Presidents; from aircraft mechanics through board chairmen of leading international business corporations." That is one postulation.

Another explanation for the absence of documentation is that on the American side, only one or two men initiated the project. They were in a position to direct others to carry out support without explaining the true purpose and they were also able to destroy their personal papers after the fact.

A similar scenario would have existed in Tokyo, but unlike our situation, Japanese civilians and armed forces stationed in the islands knew and *did* talk about the Earhart affair, among themselves at least. Later we would interview a Marshallese who had been "coffee maker" for Japanese officers at their headquarters on Jaluit. He said the Japanese talked of little else for days.

Neither explanation for official silence on both sides of the ocean is wholly satisfactory but that seems to be characteristic of this case. The search is also interesting because of the conditions under which it was conducted. All

was not as efficient as the *Lexington* report might indicate.
While there were likely several demonstrations of courage
and determination, such as the extremely hazardous
attempt by a Navy PBY patrol plane to penetrate severe
weather in an effort to reach the scene, one individual
stands out--the commander of the Coast Guard cutter
Itasca.

Commander Warner Thompson was highly responsible
in the beginning. He repeatedly dispatched messages in an
attempt to establish firm, mutually understood radio proce-
dure. He correctly recognized that radio communication
and direction finding were essential. He organized his crew,
placing an additional emergency direction finder on shore
at Howland to cope with any contingency. But his efforts
went largely unheeded. By July 1 (Howland time) he still
did not know what communication facilities Amelia planned
to utilize nor the capability of her equipment. He was to
learn of her actual departure and estimated flight time via a
newscast. Despite these handicaps, Thompson's crew made
every effort to salvage a mission which was in trouble from
the time it left the ground. Sooner than two hours after
radio contact was lost, Commander Thompson commenced
search activity at his own initiative, in a direction indicated
by meager information from Earhart. Unfortunately
Thompson's well conceived plans were not carried out
exactly as he had envisioned.

FROM: USCG *ITASCA*

TO: CMDR SAN FRANCISCO DIV CG

WE HAVE HAD NO POSITIONS COMMA SPEED
COMMA OR COURSES FROM EARHARTS
PLANE EXCEPT SO CALLED LINE OF POSI-
TION AT 0800 WHICH HAD NO REFERENCE
POINT PERIOD SHE GAVE US NONE OF HER
BEARINGS PERIOD BELIEVE SHE PASSED TO
NORTH AND WEST OF ISLAND ABOUT 0800
AND MISSED IT IN THE GLARE OF RISING
SUN THOUGH WE WERE SMOKING HEAVILY
AT THAT TIME PERIOD JUDGE SHE CAME

DOWN BETWEEN 237 AND 90 FROM HOW-
LAND AND WITHIN 100 MILES PERIOD HAVE
BROADCAST AS INDICATED 1402

The *Itasca* was joined by Navy ships from Hawaii but
without an overall search plan, each proceeded according to
theories of the individual commanders. Five full days later
the aircraft carrier *Lexington* was dispatched from her
berth at Los Angeles and a coordinated search plan went
into operation.

When I attempted to catalogue an accurate count of
wireless messages provided the *Itasca* and later the
Lexington, I became overwhelmed. A representative sam-
pling follows: excerpts of routine radio traffic containing
other messages are included in Appendix C.

*[Although the "cablease" used in radio transmissions may
prove unintelligible to lay readers, all messages are quoted
verbatim in the interests of accuracy.]*

FROM: SANFRANCISCO DIVISION

TO: *ITASCA*

8005 FOLLOWING FOR CONSIDERATION
COLON CHECKING REPORTS RECEIVED AT
0555 PST ON 3105 KC 3 JULY CONSIDERABLE
BELIEF IN ONE REPORT WHICH STATED
WOMANS VOICE MADE FOUR DISTRESS
CALLS FOLLOWED BY KHAQQ FOLLOWED ON
KEY BY 280 GARBLED OFF HOWLAND
BATTERY VERY WEAK CANT LAST LONG
OTHER GARBLED INDICATED SAND OR BANK
PERIOD ONLY BANKS CHARTED ARE SOUTH
AND EAST OF HOWLAND HOWEVER REPORT
MAY HAVE BEEN 224 NNW OF HOWLAND
INVESTIGATING FURTHER

AM EMBASSY LONDON (ENGLAND)
DEPARTMENTS 328, JULY 30
WITH REFERENCE TO THE REQUEST THAT A
BOAT FROM THE GILBERT ISLANDS MAKE A

THOROUGH SURFACE SEARCH FOR AMELIA
EARHART AT MR. PUTNAM'S EXPENSE
COMMA THE LATTER NOW URGES THAT AN
IMMEDIATE SEARCH BE BEGUN OF FOLLOW-
ING POSITION COLON 174 DEGREES TEN
MINUTES EAST LONG TWO DEGREES THIRTY
SIX MIN N LAT PERIOD THIS ONLY 85 MILES
FROM TARAWA ON MAKING ISLAND
BEARING THENCE 106 DEGREES TRUE
PERIOD MR PUTNAM BELIEVES HE HAS
APPARENTLY AUTHENTIC INFORMATION
FROM FORMER COMMANDER COPRA VESSEL
SUBSTANTIATED BY RELIABLE AMERICAN
THAT UNCHARTED REEF EXISTS AT THAT
POINT WHICH IS FREQUENTLY VISITED FOR
TURTLE EGGS COMMA OT COTORA COMMA
BY OLDER GILBERTESE NATIVES PERIOD HE
BELIEVES THAT CAPT I HANDLEY OF
TARAWA KNOWS ABOUT IT PERIOD PLEASE
EXPEDITE REPLY
HULL

8005 PAN AMERICAN AIRWAYS THROUGH
COLONEL YOUNG REPORT RADIO BEARING
ON PLANE SIGNAL MORNING FIFTH AS ONE
FOUR FOUR DEGREES FROM WAKE ISLAND
AND ARE REASONABLY CERTAIN OF
BEARING PERIOD POSSIBILITY INTER-
SECTION POSITION LINE GIVEN JUST
BEFORE LAST PLANE TRANSMISSION AND
LATITUDE LINE 281 MILES NORTH OF HOW-
LAND USING HOWLAND AS REFERENCE
POINT MAY BE PLANES POSITION BEARING
FROM WAKE ISLAND PLACES PLANE NEAR
LINE OF POSITION AND INTERSECTION OF
RADIO BEARINGS FROM WAKE AND HONO-
LULU GIVE INDICATION OF POSITION
PHOENIX GROUP PERIOD WHICH FURTHER
AAA SUBSTANTIATED AA WHO FEEL PLANES

RADIO COULD FUNCTION ONLY ON SHORE

WESTERN UNION
ADMIRAL WILLIAM LEAHY CHIEF NAVAL
OPERATIONS
CAN YOU ASCERTAIN POSSIBLY CONFI-
DENTIALLY EXACTLY WHAT JAPANESE ARE
DOING OR WILL DO STOP CERTAIN INFOR-
MATION AND ESPECIALLY DEDUCTIONS
FROM WEATHER ANALYSIS MAKE ME EAGER
FOR SEARCH REGION WEST OF HOWLAND
VICINITY OF LONGITUDE 180 AND WESTERLY
ESPECIALLY APPROACHING GILBERT
ISLAND AND GENERALLY NORTHWESTERLY
STOP STRONG WESTERLY DRIFT THAT
REGION STOP PERHAPS JAPANESE WILLING
TO TACKLE THAT TERRITORY WHICH IN
DIRECTION THEIR MANDATE STOP MEAN-
TIME OBVIOUSLY RADIO SIGNALS IF
AUTHENTIC SUBSTANTIATE WISDOM NAVY
SEARCH SOUTHEASTWARD AS PROGRESS-
ING GRATEFULLY
G P PUTNAM

WESTERN UNION
ADMIRAL WILLIAM LEAHY CHIEF NAVAL
OPERATIONS
DEEPLY GRATEFUL STEPS BE TAKEN TO
SEARCH AREA SLIGHTLY NORTH OF INTER-
SECTION OF LONGITUDE 170 EAST AND
EQUATOR CONTEMPORANEOUSLY WITH
SEARCH OF GILBERT ISLAND STOP BECAUSE
PECULIAR INTIMATE NATURE ALLEGED
INFORMATION THIS IS A CONFIDENTIAL
PERSONAL REQUEST TO YOU STOP MOST
COMPELLING UNUSUAL CIRCUMSTANCES
DICTATE ALTHOUGH SOLE OBVIOUS REA-
SONABLENESS LIES IN WESTWARD PREVAIL-

ING DRIFT WHICH MIGHT WELL HAVE
CARRIED FLOATING PLANE THROUGH
GILBERTS TO DESIGNATED AREA STOP ANY-
WAY CANNOT PASS UP THIS BET FORLORN
AS IT MAY BE

GEORGE PALMER PUTNAM

These are but a few of the unofficial reported intercepts
from all over the world. No one could fault Putnam for the
heavy hand he wielded, but the myriad of directions must
have been a frustrating distraction to the search commanders. Thompson later expressed himself in bitter tones: "If
only someone would have *listened* to me. The whole thing
was so *unnecessary!*"

So the official search ended on a note of angry
frustration. Almost 50 years after the fact, doubts still assail
Earhart researchers. Could I possibly unearth anything new
after all these years? I was going to try.

Map of Saipan

U.S. Naval Oceanographic Office

Chapter Eight:
THE TEAM

It was time to go to work. I was weary of reading musty
documents and chasing down people to interview. I would
get a search team together, decide what equipment was
needed and head out.

My hypothesis pointed to the Marshall Islands. I was
convinced that Earhart had agreed to overfly territory
north of her course. Whether she actually *did* was immate-
rial, but if she had, it could well have put her in that
vicinity of the Marshalls. It was the only area not searched
by our ships. Ray's theory about flight conditions put her
short of her dead reckoning position; the Marshalls represented the nearest land. Then there was Tanaki. He
believed an American airplane had gone down nearby and I
believed him. We would start on the island of Majuro.

In contemplating teammates, I decided someone with an
understanding of how to organize travel and equipment for
such an expedition would be valuable. I immediately
thought of Michael Harris. I had met Mike in 1979 in
Boston when he returned from the first attempt to locate
the *Titanic*. Mike lives for adventure; his energy and
enthusiasm are boundless. He is never happier than when
probing some Godforsaken desert or jungle for secrets. His
projects are as big as his ambition. Other than the *Titanic*
expedition, he directed the documentary film *Deadly
Fathoms*, an eerie trip under the waters off Bikini Atoll. His
camera probed inside ships deliberately sunk by atomic
bomb blasts during tests conducted in the late '40s. The

hangar deck of the sunken carrier *Saratoga* is shown to contain aircraft, their bombs still in place. Mike was with an expedition to Mt. Ararat in search of Noah's Ark. The logo on his letterhead reads <u>Producer - Director Expedition Leader</u>, which pretty well sums up Michael Harris. He would be the perfect advisor/associate, if I could first find and then convince him. Mike maintains an office but he can never be found there. When I finally tracked him down, he seemed interested. We would talk more, he said, when he returned from some mysterious trip he wouldn't discuss.

With his participation far from certain, I moved to other possible team members; the search would involve dozens of interviews. I recalled Ben Berry's words of caution: Not all islanders were eager to talk to Americans. Who would be most effective in questioning recalcitrant witnesses? A lawyer seemed logical and I penciled in the name Tom Brennan III immediately below Mike Harris.

Our trip warranted recording on film the people, places, documents and artifacts we would discover. I wanted people with me that I knew, and I turned to Dick Huntoon, my long-time friend who had accompanied me on the first trip. Dick had shrewd insight and I felt his presence on this trip was essential.

I was highly pleased with my selections, and next began itemizing preparations and equipment. We could be under-way in less than a month, I calculated. It had never occurred to me that anyone could resist the lure of hieing off on a Pacific adventure, but I found a couple right away. Tom was adamant; he was far too busy, could never make arrangements for an associate to take over on short notice. He would try, but it could be weeks, even months. Dick's reaction was much the same. Busy, busy, Buddy. Don't see any way. He also added a blunt, "You're off your gourd. There aren't a handful of people alive who even know who the woman was. I'd bet that airplane broke into a hundred pieces when it crashed. You'd have to walk over the bottom of half the Pacific to find all the parts."

I got stubborn; I needed those two. I hadn't been in the real estate business all those years without learning a little bit about making a hard sell. I plotted.

A few weeks later, seated in a semi-circle facing me were Tom Brennan III, Dick Huntoon and Michael Harris. The purpose--first briefing on The Search For Amelia Earhart. I had been especially lucky to snare Mike. He had approval from the Philippine government to film the story of guerilla warfare there during World War II.* He would take a "few of his people" on our trip. It represented an opportunity for him to get some stock jungle footage. He remembered from his trip to the Marshalls to do *Deadly Fathoms* that a number of Japanese lived there. Perhaps he could hire some as extras.

My speech was well rehearsed. I stood in front of the wall map and gave them the full conclusions from my hours of research, including why I believed our search should start in the Marshalls. When I finally sat down, there was a long silence. Dick was the first one to speak.

"Buddy, what are we *really* looking for, the airplane or the crew?"

"Both, Dick. If we find one, we have a good chance of finding both. But first priority is to try and trace the movements of Earhart and Noonan."

"Since you roped me into this thing," Dick continued, "I decided to do some background research. As I read Fred Goerner's book, something occurred to me. The Japanese were regular sponges then in the matter of copying designs and specifications. The *Electra* had many of our newest designs incorporated, like the engines, radios, lightweight metal alloys. It probably could outperform any twin-engine Japanese airplane of the period. If they had gotten their hands on it, you can believe they would have taken it apart piece by piece. And after examining those pieces they would undoubtedly try to reassemble it and fly it. That would have been a major intelligence coup!

"On his own expedition, Goerner discovered a generator

* Mike's dealings were with President Ferdinand Marcos. As far as I know, he was never able to complete the project.

of Japanese manufacture, not from the *Electra*. But when he took that generator to the Bendix people, their first reaction was that it had come from an old E-5 model. It took much detailed lab work to establish that the bearings were made in Japan and that it had metric threading. The same was true with the starter motor he found. Didn't it strike anyone as odd that these were virtual carbon copies of parts installed on Earhart's airplane? My theory is that if the Japanese had found that airplane, they would have taken it away to strip and study it. Where did they have facilities to do that? Very likely a long way from where they went down."

I regarded Dick with new respect. The others were nodding in agreement. Now we had two different search patterns! Everyone agreed that our first priority would be discovering the fate of the two flyers, but that we would keep alert to any leads regarding the airplane.

Tom spoke. "Everything you're saying seems to point toward capture by the Japanese Army. Now I've been doing some reading myself about prewar conditions in the Pacific, and this question bothers me: 'Why didn't the Japanese just release Earhart and Noonan and send them home?' Even if they believed them to be on a spy mission, you'd think they'd be yelling 'Foul!' 'Imperialistic Americans spying on poor Japan'--expose us to the whole world. I can picture them parading their captives down the main street of Tokyo, beating confessions out of them. So what you're theorizing, Dick, may be a part of the answer--they wanted to examine that airplane without us knowing about it.

But from what I read, we'd be crediting the Japanese with organized logic and reasoning they didn't have at that time. Two factions were doing a bit of infighting on the home front. The militant faction was laying plans to expand into Southeast Asia. A moderate faction, including some senior military people, were saying, 'We can never get away with such a thing.'

"The Marshalls were the 'boondocks' as far as military assignments were concerned. The planned expansion route went straight south. The Marshalls, almost 2,000 miles

east, would only serve as a buffer against United States
intervention. It's unlikely that Japan's crack troops and
commanders would have been relegated to such unim-
portant duty.

"So here's a probable scenario. The Japanese commander in the Marshalls is confronted by a beaming aide
who tells him, 'We have captured two American spies and
their plane!' The Colonel might well reason that if he plays
this right, he could be transferred off this Godforsaken
island!' The flyers are hustled off to jail for interrogation
where it is discovered the pilot is a woman! How do you
treat a woman spy? A few days pass in contemplation of
protocol. Finally word filters up to supreme headquarters
that Amelia Earhart is being held prisoner in the Marshall
Islands.

"This creates a small problem, for in the meantime,
their diplomats have gravely assured the Americans that
they know nothing and are out searching their territory. To
announce later that she had been a prisoner all along would
be to lose face, something the Japanese just don't do. It
looks to me as if Earhart and Noonan were shot and the
evidence buried for no other reason than to save face! I
agree with Dick about the airplane. After they finished
examining and copying, it went the same route as the crew."

Tom's was not a cheerful outlook. I turned to Mike who
had been a thoughtful listener thus far. "You know," he
began, "I believe we stand a better chance than before to get
the islanders to talk freely. Americans are more readily
accepted now. In the '60s when Goerner was there for
example, distrust for Americans was at an all time high.
Klaas, Loomis, and Strippel were also hampered by this
aversion to volunteering information. If we approach the
natives right, I'll bet we can persuade people to talk that
have never been known to have information about the
disappearance. And this is important--they're the only *new*
sources we have. With the unlikely exception of discovering
unrevealed classified American or Japanese documents, the
people who were on the islands at the time are our best
hope of original sources. This makes it essential to ask

questions in the right way."

"I picked up quite a bit of the local culture when I was
there shooting the Bikini project. You're dealing with
people who have lived with unwelcome landlords for almost
three centuries. Before that, these people were fierce
fighters. Magellan stopped in the Marshalls on his trip
around the world, but didn't stay long. His crew dubbed the
place 'Islands of The Thieves.' The islanders were adven-
turers. They would set off on trips of a thousand miles in
canoes. An old man showed me how they navigated--lined
up some sticks in the sand to represent ocean currents.
Then put down a shell and crossed the sticks. The shell
represented an island. Where the sticks (current) rejoined
after being diverted by the island, the waves assumed a
distinct pattern. When you saw this unique wave pattern,
you knew where you were. They memorized these patterns
and handed the knowledge down to the young men.

"But as I say, three centuries of living under the thumb
of four major world powers has left its mark. First the
Spaniards, back in the 1500s, who shipped the entire native
population of the Marianas to Guam at the same time they
were importing Christianity. Next came the Germans, all
business in copra, but every bit as harsh where the natives
were concerned. After the Germans lost World War I, the
Marshalls, Marianas and Carolines were mandated to Japan
for 'protection.' Their occupation wasn't as bad as is
commonly thought, though. Some close ties were made and
a lot of pro-Japanese feeling exists today, as Ben Berry told
you. Then came benevolent old Uncle Sam to save them
from the big bad Japanese. We set them free and showed
them how to be a democracy.

"But 300 years of occupation has changed these people.
A psychologist explained to me that the capacity to express
anger has been bred out of them because it's just too
dangerous. This leads to another unusual cultural orien-
tation. In many countries, the native population has gone
'underground' during an occupation. Information passes
freely among them; resistance is organized. Not so the
Marshallese. They evolved into a highly secretive people.

Do not confide in your neighbor; face is important. Do not put yourself in a position to be ridiculed or criticized. The Marshallese are reluctant to accept or give orders. The traditional rulers mediate; not govern. Our efforts to introduce democracy created something of a schism here. Two types of leadership have emerged. The traditional tribal leader, the *Alab*, is respected for knowledge and offers advice. The political leaders deal with law. You need to understand some of these things before we go barging in there demanding answers and throwing our weight around. We'll just have to probe gently to find out when we go to government and when we go to the Queen, etc.

Mike's little history lesson was a revelation. I realized that I had not *known* those people I talked with on my first trip. I was gaining new admiration for my teammates. We were going to be successful; I could feel it. I could see enthusiasm building in the others too.

The conversation turned to logistics--what to take, who would be responsible for what. We discussed dates and finally settled on the middle of November. At last I was seeing some ACTION!

Then a real blow. Just a few weeks before departure, Dick cancels. Pressing business matters make the trip impossible. I understand. Mike and Tom can take care of the photography but I will miss Dick. I know he is disappointed also. After our first trip, he wanted badly to be in on the follow-up.

****

Extracts from the Journal of Tom Brennan III

November 1, 1983:
So I'm going to the Marshall Islands. Why? I don't really want to go, I think. Even after hearing the others talk this afternoon, I can't really believe Buddy is going to find anything out there. But I can't let anyone know I have doubts. I agreed to go and I'll give it everything I've got. I think I like Mike Harris; he seems to know what he's doing.

Break the news to Nancy. I haven't told her I was going for certain yet. Not looking forward to that one.

Things to do/get:
camera lens--big carrying case
medical kit--lots of paregoric or kaopectate;
go to bank--increase Amer Express limit!
mosquito net, snake bite kit? Buddy says no snakes there--in that jungle??? I wonder????
Look up diet for tropics. Bet food is lousy plus high carb.

November 8:
Read more on the islands and people. A good steer Mike gave us on how to ask questions there. Not like in a courtroom! Permits and things. Must bone up on their laws--where? Unloaded last of my pending stuff today. Good feeling but God---just hope there are no screw ups! What if I lose a big client while I'm off chasing dusky maidens along moonlit beaches?

November 14:
Last day before leap off! Guess I'm as ready as I'll ever be. We meet Mike and entourage in LA. Understand his son writes for one of the daytime soaps there. Interesting. Okay, admit it Brennan. You're getting excited! A chance, perhaps, to observe history being made! How many chances like that does the ordinary guy get? Earlier concern about Buddy making this trip so soon after surgery is gone. The guy thrives on activity!

Chapter Nine:

THE SECOND EXPEDITION - MAJURO

Even from my lofty perch at 39,000 feet, the Pacific Ocean was, with its endless expanse, nothing less than awesome. Slouched in a comfortably upholstered seat, temperature a controlled 72 degrees, sound of the DC-10's powerful engines muted by protective insulation, a recent movie running, it was easy to lose sight of potential hazards. I recalled Ray's vivid description of what Earhart and Noonan must have endured that tragic night. Hard to believe.

The captain had announced that we would be about five hours between LA and Honolulu. A routine flight; maybe a hundred planes a day back and forth. Not a square foot of land in sight! I dredged up a bit of trivia--of the area we call the Pacific Ocean, less than one percent is solid land. I looked outside and wondered, "Do any of these pilots ever get lost, like Amelia?" I soon had an opportunity to find out. One of the pilots came by on his obligatory PR trip. "Never gotten lost on one of these trips yet," he answered, in response to my apparently anxious question. I then explained that I was doing research on Amelia Earhart's disappearance and inquired as to what kind of navigation equipment he had that she didn't. He was immediately interested, took the adjoining seat and began explaining modern navigational devices. One allowed you to set your desired track and couple it to the auto pilot. Radar-type impulses instructed the auto pilot which way to correct the heading. The radios on board (single side band he called them) allowed the crew to talk to Honolulu or the mainland all the way across the ocean, practically static free. Then he began asking about my project.

Ahead of me, Mike was sound asleep. This was old stuff to him. Across the aisle, Tom was talking earnestly with Mike's photographer, a youngster named NIK. They seemed to hit it off from the first introduction. Clad in loose colorful sport shirts and loafers we didn't exactly typify the intrepid exploration team, I thought wryly. I extracted my notebook and reviewed what we planned to do.

Ben Berry had been alerted to meet us at Majuro. We would need all his considerable talent. First we would make a round of the government offices. I knew some changes had occurred since I was last there, something to do with a new constitution. Above all we would need government support. President Kabua would be my first call and then I would visit with Tanaki. We had brought a video mini-cam and planned to get as much of this on tape as possible. How would these people talk and react when we placed them in front of a camera? We would just have to take things as they came.

Shortly the first of the Hawaiian Islands became visible, their higher peaks poking into the ever-present afternoon rain clouds. Moments later we rolled to a halt at the Honolulu air terminal. Hawaii is the visitor's first introduction to the seductive nature of this unique climate of "soft" air. The temperature is frequently in the low 80s with a pleasant breeze. In spite of yourself, a gradual lassitude envelopes you. Our connecting flight is two hours late, but here things run on "Micronesian Time"--"I'll do it if I say I'll do it, but maybe not today."

Eventually we board our 727 for the flight to Majuro. I'm brought back to the business aspect of our trip almost immediately. To my surprise and delight Amata Kabua, President of the Republic of the Marshall Islands, is seated across the aisle--a heaven sent opportunity to lay the groundwork for our mission. Even better, his First Secretary, Oscar de Brum, is Tom's seatmate. I want desperately to brief Tom on some questions to ask but I know it would be a mistake.

President Kabua remembers me and soon I am chatting with the distinguished looking head of government. I sense he is tired. In response to polite questions he tells me he has been in Honolulu attending a conference with American officials. Many details remain to be resolved in the transfer of administrative powers to the Republic under terms of the new Compact of Free Association. I express interest and soon he is providing details of the local situation which we need very much to know.

That he is dedicated to the betterment of his people is readily apparent. An earnest expression on his *cafe au lait* features, he taps my knee with a well-manicured finger to emphasize points. His eyes are serious behind wire rimmed spectacles. His major concern is the matter of economic self sufficiency.

President Kabua does not hesitate to blame Americans for many of the problems he faces. "I do a great deal of traveling, Mr. Brennan. I was educated in American schools and understand Americans. I realize that your actions to help Micronesians have the loftiest motives; but your efforts have been largely in the form of direct cash payments for welfare programs. Our people quickly develop a dependence upon whatever is provided. We do not yet fully understand or appreciate your principles of free enterprise. For example, our readily accessible fishing waters, the lagoons, are fished out. But a few miles further out, the Japanese use large "fishing factories" to catch tuna in abundance. We buy that tuna, caught in our territorial waters, after it has been taken to Japan and canned, which makes us net importers of our own fish, Mr. Brennan.

"Our sole export just now is copra. On our list of imports, I'm sorry to say, alcoholic beverages are in third place, exceeded only by textiles and building materials. Working in government created jobs (about 50 per cent of all employment) is prestigious. Working for another man is demeaning. This is one reason we do not have a large scale commercial fishing industry. Self employment is negligible, consisting largely of taxicab operation.

"We are in a time of great opportunity, Mr. Brennan. America is most generous; we are granted complete powers of self-government. The United States guarantees our security and defense. An annual payment to our government provides $755 per citizen over 15 years of age. Forty per cent of that is earmarked for economic development. A long way to go, but the opportunity is there."

I was impressed with this man and wished him every success. I turned to the purpose of our expedition, reminding him of the start he had given us during our previous trip. "Mr. President, above all we want to observe every protocol while carrying out our search. I know Americans have a bad habit of ignoring local customs and creating bad feelings. Can you help us avoid doing this?

"You refer to the position the Royal Family holds in our society. The title of King or Queen stems from a single clan; succession is by birthright. The ruler of individual islands holds titular ownership of all land and receives a portion of all revenues derived therefrom. Removal of the old airplanes we discussed last year is a good example. To do this you must first obtain an export permit from our government. The next step is to obtain permission from (in this case) Queen Bosquet of Mili. We will presume she is the owner of the land where the airplanes are located. If another person is operating, say, a coconut harvesting business on this land, arrangements would be made with him."

He smiled at my confused expression. "But you are now concerned with finding people who may have knowledge of the Earhart disappearance and are willing to talk about it. Here we encounter another hierarchy--the island chieftains. The local clan chief, the *Alab*, is loyal to a larger chief, the *Iroij*. They are, in turn, loyal to the *Iroij Laplap*, Chief of Chiefs. You are wise to understand this somewhat complex structure before you start. The people you question will probably seek the advice of these chieftains. You will never know it, but a negative endorsement from any one of them will mean your potential witness can remember nothing."

An amused twinkle in his eyes he concluded, "I am very conscious of the influence exerted by this structure. I inherited the title of *Iroij* prior to entering politics, and am one of the few to make the transition. My reelection may well depend upon their support. Now, if you will excuse me Mr. Brennan, there are a few matters I wish to discuss with First Secretary de Brum before we land. Please call on me any time during your stay in the Marshalls. I wish you every success."

Mike couldn't wait to pump me for details of my conversation with President Kabua. We were both elated at how easily we had solved the problem of how to proceed. With Ben Berry to smooth the way for us, we were bound to find new sources of information.

The captain announced our landing at Johnson Island, and we were soon rolling down a long concrete runway lined with neat, well-ordered buildings--a full American military layout guarded like Fort Knox. In blunt terms we were told that nobody, but nobody, could deplane without orders to enter the island.

****

Extracted from the Journal of T. C. Brennan III

> November 16:
> *Enroute Honolulu to Majuro. What a break! Seatmate is none other than Oscar de Brum, First Secretary to the President of The Republic of the Marshall Islands! Fascinating guy. Asked about the name. Seems he is descendent of one of the European families big in the Marshalls before Japan took over in about 1914. I mentioned our reason for going to Majuro. He remarked almost offhandedly, "Oh there's no question they went down in the Marshalls. Lot's of people saw them. The Japanese hustled them off somewhere--probably their headquarters on Saipan." I almost fell off my seat! Here was a top man in the government confirming*

*what we had come prepared to pry out of people! I
asked him why it wasn't more widely publicized. He
sort of laughed and told me, "We wonder why you
people pursue the matter. It's over and done with.
You see, a difference between Marshallese and
Americans--we want to forget those days. Earhart
and Noonan were just two more casualties among
thousands."*

*What to do? This is important stuff--should be
recorded. Will he say this all later on camera? I
don't even dare take notes! I probe some more. Do
you know people who might talk with us, people
who know what happened? He just shrugged and
said, "Oh I'm sure we can find some. Not all that
many left, you know, who actually saw anything.
Most of it has been passed down to their children
and the like." Land at Johnson Island. Clearly an
all American military installation, with remote
cameras and armed guards. Big surprise to me;
didn't know we were still on a war footing any place
in the Pacific! Ask de Brum. He says U.S. won't
even tell the Marshallese government what they're
doing. Sounds sort of huffy about it. Do I detect just
a hint of anti-Americanism here? I'll back off. Talk
to the team about how to approach him later.*

Friday, November 17, *but still same day. Crossed
International Date Line in flight. We're on the
ground at Majuro. A huge crowd swarms onto the
field as we park. Don't tell me our little expedition is
attracting attention! Turns out they are there to
meet the President. Off with the mountain of
baggage. Swarming teenagers are hauling it away
in every direction; will we ever see any of it again?
It all turns up to my surprise. We pile into an
assortment of vehicles and head for the Eastern
Gateway, our home for the next four or five days.
This whole island is a mess! Junk, piles of it--
rusting cars, empty beer cans and piles of just about*

*anything you can mention. Few paved roads, mostly
what I guess is crushed coral. Buddy and Mike
tried to prepare me but I just can't believe it. The
hotel is likewise pretty unbelievable. Divide up the
luggage and find rooms. Big sign: WATER 5 TO 7
P.M. Welcome to the Pearl of the Pacific!*

Chapter Ten:
ON THE TRAIL

It was difficult to curb my impatience that first morning. We had traveled this distance to talk with people and I wanted to get started but discretion prevailed. Mike and I, led by Ben Berry, started our round of officials. Mike wanted to do filming on the north end. This evoked much interest and while no hint of disapproval was presented, each stop required about 30 minutes of polite conversation.

My mention of intending to question persons about the fate of Amelia Earhart created little excitement. Oh yes, they had been, according to the reciter, shot down by Japanese fighters, rescued from the open sea, and picked up on one of the islands. None of the people with whom we talked were old enough to have had personal knowledge, however. I contented myself with talking to anyone I could.

I was more interested in contacting some of the "chieftains" President Kabua had described. I had a hunch that they were a much more lucrative source than the workers in government offices. Ben, naturally, knew exactly where to find the local *Alab*. A short drive up the coast in our rented car brought us to a secluded cove. There, stretched out in the shade of an outrigger canoe, hat propped over his face, was our man. He didn't seem to resent our having disturbed his midmorning nap. Ben, interpreting for us, explained to the middle-aged chief that we wished to talk to any of the islanders who were old enough to remember Amelia Earhart. A great deal of desultory conversation followed between the two, a courtesy, I knew, which must precede talk of any substance.

Mike and I expressed interest in the canoe. What was he doing to it? The native canoes are beautiful, amazing, and can really move. Named *Flying Prao* by early European explorers, these 25-30-foot craft can reach speeds of 25 M.P.H. Typical construction has an "outrigger" on one side, held in place with poles lashed to the main hull. The hull is flat on the side facing the outrigger and rounded on the windward side. The mast is placed exactly amidships and can be tilted toward either bow or stern. This simple arrangement allows the outrigger to remain balanced, stay downwind and eliminates tacking into the wind. The chieftain explained that he was repainting the hull in vivid reds and blues. He was highly pleased at our interest in the primitive craft and spent another half-hour describing its virtues. No wonder this man was so proud of his canoe; it was truly a work of art.

As we said goodbye and returned to the car, I noticed a green Datsun parked nearby, rust only beginning to make its inevitable appearance. The *Alab* was not poverty stricken I decided. When asked what they had talked about, Ben only shrugged. "Just island talk. It would not befit his position to give you information directly. He likes you though and you can bet he will tell anyone who asks that you are people to be trusted. That's all we wanted."

Our diplomatic approach paid dividends almost immediately. Over lunch we were told that an old man was willing to talk to the "American Film People." We were to hear this term frequently during our quest. I'm not certain the island people understood that we were engaged in historical research. They saw American movies and television and I think most believed we were making a feature film. History of the war era is of little interest to them.

Tom and I went over our interview outline. We had no idea what information this man possessed but we knew our priorities. We wanted to establish that the plane did go down in the islands, that Earhart and Noonan survived the landing, and that they had become prisoners of the Japanese. The old man had prepared himself for the interview with a freshly ironed shirt and trousers and wore the customary thong sandals. Ben determined that his name was Eliu Jibambam. He spoke English so I decided to conduct the interview. I thanked him for seeing us and indulged in the obligatory small talk before asking the first serious question.

"Mr. Jibambam, did you actually *see* the Americans believed to be Amelia Earhart and Fred Noonan? Were they here on Majuro?"

"No, no, not see. They not on Majuro. On Jaluit, I think. I know from friend then, before the war. This friend is Japanese. We visit, he has Japanese beer, we talk you know."

I was a bit confused. "Did you speak Japanese, Mr. Jibambam, or did your friend speak English?"

"Oh no! Not English! Nobody speak English around Japanese. Japanese cut off head any person speaking English. Say they American spy person. Many people here killed for being spy. No, we speak Japanese, all time."

"What did your friend tell you about the two Americans, Mr. Jibambam?"

"He ask if I hear about two American spies they capture. Other people have told me, but I tell my friend 'No, I do not hear'."

"Why would he ask you if you knew?"

"Japanese very pleased to capture spies. It is very big thing for them."

"Well, did he tell you their names?"

"No, no name. Only say that one spy is woman. Japanese think very strange that Americans use woman spy."

"I see. How old were you when you talked with your friend, Mr. Jibambam?"

"Oh young man then. Now I am 72."

"Yes. Well what year would this have been?"

"Before war comes. Several years. My friend he works for company in Japan that does building. He goes to many islands to make the concrete."

I hated to put words in the old man's mouth but I had to get a better fix on the date. "Would this have been as early as, say, 1936, '37, 1940?"

"Yes, before war it was."

And that was to be the extent of Eliu Jibambam's
testimony. This vague concept of dates was to plague us
throughout. In this place where today is a time of little
interest and concern, tomorrow of much less and yesterday
of none whatsoever, a serious historian would throw up his
hands. We adjourned to a place Tom and NIK had
discovered the day before, the Lanai Club, to critique our
first interview. The Lanai had unquestionable atmosphere--
last night's cigarette smoke, stale beer and fish. The sounds
of a noisy pool game and pinging of electronic poker games
could just be heard over the emissions of 400-watt stereo
speakers.

I was disappointed by the little we had learned from
Jibambam. I guess I had wanted our first interview to
produce something new and sensational. Mike took a more
optimistic view. "Look, first of all this guy approached us.
You just don't realize how unusual that is. He'll tell others
that we treated him okay. This interview will lead to others,
just wait and see. Another thing--he didn't give us a wild
yarn, information he knew we wanted to hear. I think he
was just trying to be helpful. I put more credence in little
bits of seemingly useless information like this than a long
story by someone with an apparently faultless memory and
an eagle eye for exact detail. If we plod along like this, we'll
get our leads; I'm confident of it. We have the people
talking freely; that's progress in itself."

But we didn't have much time for "plodding" I told
myself, and at the same time knew we couldn't rush
matters. We turned to discussing ways of getting the
Japanese fellow, Amaron, to talk with us. This was really
frustrating. Ben had tried approaching him through one of
the local policemen, a close acquaintance of Amaron's.
(Remember you don't just walk up to someone and start
talking; things must be "arranged.") Ben reported that
Amaron still had family in Japan and was concerned that
his story would reflect on them.

I couldn't believe that. First of all he *had* told his story to others at least twice. What possible repercussion could his story set off after 50 years? Perhaps going on camera was scaring him. We rejected the idea of having an informal, off-the-record talk though. If he had, as he had told others, actually seen and talked with Amelia and Fred Noonan, it was crucial testimony. I wanted it documented down to the last comma. Besides I wanted a firsthand opportunity to judge his veracity. Ben said he would keep trying.

We completed our first day's work by getting Tanaki to tell his story on camera. He had nothing to add to what he had told me previously. His friend, a crewman on board the Japanese ship *Koshu*, told him the ship had been ordered, on very short notice, to search for an American airplane which had crashed. The shy old man was very convincing on camera.

Mike talked with the owner of the Lanai and offered to show his film *Deadly Fathoms* there in a couple of nights. We decided to make a special invitation to President Kabua and First Secretary de Brum. Mike also arranged to appear on a local radio talk show, hoping to expose our search to the public and demonstrate the high level of interest in our project.

The next day, Saturday, would be busy. Sunday was an election day, with little else happening on the island. We planned to hold three taping sessions on Saturday. A Mr. John Heinie had agreed to discuss his memories of the airplane and Lotan Jack had information from a period when he worked for the Japanese. We planned to leave time in case Amaron decided to talk to us. I turned in early, tired but down. Jet lag, I told myself. Before I drifted off to sleep I realized that I really liked the two old men we had talked with today. For the first time, the islanders were coming alive, as real and interesting people.

****

Extracts from the Journal of T. C. Brennan III

November 19:
Up early, fully recuperated from the trip. Break-
fast across the street from our hotel in a 24-hour
place, The Island Hostess. Eggs and bacon pass-
able. Dick had prepared me for starvation. After last
night's experience in the shower, may do like the
islanders and use the lagoon. Shower and commode
in same 3 x 5 cubicle. Water from shower rinses
everything accumulated on the stool down the
drain, crossing your feet in the process.

Took a stroll while waiting for others. Lots of
islanders up and about, all squatting in the woods,
the reef, wherever, taking their morning consti-
tutionals. Wandered off the main road into barrio
district, followed by a half-dozen kids. Watching me
pick up some sea shells, they overwhelmed me with
their offerings. Mike's sociology lesson was right.
The young ones, ten and under, are happy and
carefree. The teenagers don't smile much, mostly
drink beer and play pool. Living conditions pretty
bad. About ten per cent of the houses made of
concrete or stucco and have electricity and running
water (when it runs). The rest are just shacks and
lean-to arrangements. Many places have graves in
front yard; kept immaculate. Fresh white paint is
unusual; better houses largely unpainted or with
peeling paint. Concrete made here uses beach sand.
High salt content causes constant leeching. Many
graves of people who died in the '40s decorated with
Coke bottles embedded in the concrete. Coke bottles
very rare and highly prized then.

Wonder about today's interviews. Nothing very
exciting yesterday. Mike and Buddy optimistic but
don't know. Earhart probably did go down around
here, but will anyone ever find out exactly what
happened? Still, our slow and easy approach is
producing results. Already people are coming up

*and offering stories. Secondhand info but interesting. Two mentioned plane was shot down. How could that be? No Jap fighter planes on Mili then. Several say plane went down in the water between Mili and Jaluit. Earhart and Noonan rescued at first by fishermen; turned over to Japanese later. Was just finishing shower(?) last night when man knocked on door and gave me a book. Said he heard we were looking for Earhart material. It was published in South Africa! The title is **Amelia Earhart — Her Last Flight**, by a writer named Skaggs. Will try to read it tonight.*

Eliu Jibambam

Lotan Jack

Chapter Eleven:
THE WITNESSES

Tom is a veritable ferret. At breakfast he told us of seeing an old Japanese fighter plane, a Zero, in a storage yard further down the island. My mind was busy with today's interviews but I couldn't resist checking it out. A few inquiries revealed that an attorney, Max Messman, represented the owners. Messman confirmed that the airplane was indeed for sale. Still smarting from my failure to obtain even *one* plane in display condition, I made arrangements to meet the man at the storage yard.

This was to be my final effort to obtain a display model. The airplane was reasonably intact or at least appeared to have been when originally placed in the yard. But mankind had managed to do what years of normal corrosion and deterioration had not--the plane was a mess. When yard workers periodically had found it necessary to move the plane to make room for other items, they had used a fork-lift. Their technique had consisted of ramming the front prongs of the fork-lift through the plane's fragile aluminum skin and it was evident that the process had been repeated several times. I left in disgust, finished with the airplane salvage business. (Well, of course, if we managed to locate that Lockheed *Electra*...)

But this side trip provided a dividend, for I discovered a plausible reason for many islanders' reluctance to discuss events which had occurred during the area's Japanese occupation. The opinion was provided with an understanding that it would not to be attributed to any one person. It

seemed their silence might be bred in the Japanese practice
of employing natives of an occupied country as internal
security. These "policemen" were not provided firearms but
used the familiar police "baton" to enforce law and order.
On the surface, the concept is a practical method to allay
the natural fears of a conquered people. But the Japanese
secret police, the *Kempeitai*, had a much deeper motive
than just instilling public trust. They knew that people
willing to collaborate with an occupying power are usually
opportunists, frequently desirous of exercising power over
people who may have rejected them in the past. These
people can be easily induced to become undercover "windows" into the local community. Plots for sabotage and
resistance are more easily detected by a local. But it seldom
takes long for these local collaborators to become generally
loathed and feared, which happened throughout the
islands. With the disappearance of their Japanese masters,
however, these little police forces found themselves distinctly unpopular with the general public. Many natives had
endured torture and deprivation or had seen friends and
family members executed under the Japanese for almost
trivial reasons. The inbred Micronesian fear of authority
figures probably saved them from mass summary execution,
the fate of many of their contemporaries in other lands.

A number of these puppet policemen are still alive, and
fear of their ability to inflict punishment still exists among
many of the less sophisticated islanders! We would
encounter this influence on two separate occasions. Hoping
that one of these former Japanese confidantes could cast
light on the fate of Amelia Earhart, we asked for an
interview, but were rebuffed in a most hostile manner!

Could this be a factor in Bilamon Amaron's persistent
refusal to see us? I thought so. Amaron although born in
the Marshalls, was Japanese. Now he is a respected
businessman, but who knows what old hatreds may lie
festering? After 50 years, did he still fear retribution by
former collaborators?

We were a few minutes late for our taped interview with
Mr. Heinie. We set up at our favorite location, a corner

table on the Lanai Club patio. Mr. Heinie would make an impressive witness. School principal, minister of the local Congregational Church and assistant trial lawyer, his statement would be a strong link in the chain we were forging. I opened the session by asking him to tell us what he knew of the Earhart affair.

"During my early life, I lived on the island of Jaluit. I attended Japanese schools there. One day, I was just entering high school I believe, the Japanese came and told us all the children were to go down to the harbor and wave little Japanese flags as a ship came into the harbor. I do not remember the name of the ship but I recall that, as we stood there waving our flags, the ship was towing a barge. On the barge was an airplane. It was partially covered but I could tell it was silver colored. It was smaller than, and did not resemble, the Japanese seaplanes we were familiar with."

"Was it a twin engine airplane?" I prompted him.

"Oh yes, it had two props. But the tail, I could not see the tail. Maybe it was missing, maybe it was covered up. I do not know what kind of airplane it was but later I was told that it was the plane an American lady had been flying when she crashed."

"Do you know where the ship went after it left Jaluit, Mr. Heinie?"

"I believe it went on to Kwajalein, that was headquarters for the Japanese Navy, then on to Truk and Saipan. Saipan was big Japanese headquarters. From there it would go to Japan I believe."

This appeared to be the extent of the man's knowledge of the "silver airplane." I asked him one more time to confirm the year as being 1937 which he did, relating the date to his year in school. I probed for details, hoping to spark another relevant disclosure. "What was life like under the Japanese, Mr. Heinie?"

The man's handsome, heavy set features remained impassive as he proceeded to relate very matter-of-factly, a chilling story of one family's tragic experience. "My grandfather came to the islands as a minister. Things went well with his congregation until the war started. Then they came and took him away. My father looked for him but he was unable to learn what had happened. Later a Japanese told me my grandfather had died. Later yet I was told he had been beheaded.

"One day I was helping my father build an air raid shelter when the Japanese soldiers came. They tell my father and me to return to our house. When we got there, we found that they had dismantled everything in the house. Stuff was sitting around in boxes. They were very interested in my father's typewriter. They did not seem to know what it was but believed it was some sort of communication device for spying. They took the typewriter with them and left.

"About two months later, the Japanese soldiers came back to our house with a Marshallese who was known to be sympathetic and was helping them. They take my father and my mother. I do not see them for several months.

"Later the Japanese come again at night and they wake me. They take me with them and throw me into the hold of a launch. I land on other people. They tell me that we are to be sent to a forced labor camp. I am allowed to see my parents one more time for about ten minutes. Then we are put to work repairing damage the bombers caused."

"This was after the war started?"

"Yes, things were not bad until the war started. Then the Japanese became very angry. They take my parents to the same spot where my grandfather was killed, and they kill them also."

"How did they die, Mr. Heinie?"

"They were beheaded."

The absence of emotion in his brief recitation of this brutal act was jarring. I found it hard to continue. The soft-spoken native went on without interruption however.

"I was still very young and they seemed to have trouble making up their minds whether to go ahead and kill me also. They put me prisoner in an air raid shelter. I was lucky. My Japanese guard was a Christian. He told me he did not want to see me killed, told me to run to the beach and escape. He would shoot over my head to make the other Japanese think he was trying to stop me. I did and swam about a mile to another island. There I found other Marshallese who were running from the Japanese. We managed to avoid capture until after the war was over."

Mr. Heinie stopped speaking, his story finished, and sat impassive. The next move was up to me and I didn't know what to say. I wasn't the only one deeply moved by this vignette. Mike and NIK, those two worldly filmmakers, had forgotten to turn off the camera. So impressed were we with John Heinie's gripping story that we almost forgot a last important question. Mike stopped me as I turned to leave. "What about the postcard?" He was referring to an earlier remark by Heinie that his grandfather had a postcard with Amelia Earhart's name on it. I returned to my seat and posed the question.

"Yes, my grandfather at one time wrote an article for the *Pacific Island Monthly*. In it was a photostat of a postcard that Amelia Earhart may have mailed from the island of Jaluit; at least that was the postmark."

I was excited. "Mr. Heinie, do you still have a copy of that?"

"No, years ago I gave it to my cousin. I do not know if he has it or not."

I was disappointed but at the same time recognized the importance of this information in placing Amelia in the Marshall Islands, alive. Was this one of the preaddressed letters she posted along her route; the promotional scheme with Gimble's Department Store? The term "postcard" could be a simple matter of confused terminology in translation, most understandable with only a photostat copy to examine. Was it possible that Earhart had managed to cajole or bribe one of her guards into smuggling one of those envelopes to the outside world? The attempt failed, obviously; the alert Japanese would have intercepted it easily, but what spunk! I began to believe that Amelia was a match for her captors. That she had survived was becoming a strong possibility.

I left that interview with John Heinie convinced that

one day during 1937 a Japanese ship had entered Jaluit
harbor towing a barge. On that barge was a wrecked
airplane not of Japanese manufacture. Heinie's sincere,
dispassionate narration, his absence of embellishment had
convinced me. The drama of his story was impossible to
capture, even on the video tape.

I was gaining new respect for Tom's ability as an
attorney. He had repeatedly explained that you build a case
from little pieces of information, bite them to test their
worth, and keep only the sound bits. These little bits of
sound evidence ultimately build to conclusive proof. I
suddenly saw where so many other Earhart researchers had
gone astray. Most had drawn sinister inferences from
negative testimony, the result of their inability to find
positive clues in the official accounts. We would find other
small bits, I was now convinced, and in the end succeed
where others had failed.

Our next interviewee, Mr. Lotan Jack, declined to come
to the Lanai Club. We would do this interview in a truly
native setting, beneath giant coconut palms overlooking the
lagoon. It was a fitting background for the quaint old man.
Lotan Jack was something of a local character. He did odd
jobs around the island, had a wide circle of friends, and a sly
sense of humor. Today he was all business.

Lotan Jack seemed to be one of the few who relished
the thought of seeing himself on film. He was dressed in his
finest clothes, as were all of our interviewees; large opaque
sunglasses completed his TV image. I had to admit that this
lean, wiry man did cut an impressive figure. He insisted on
conducting the interview in English although his command
of the tongue was marginal. I had expressed doubt regarding the accuracy of his story but Oscar de Brum assured us
the old man was credible.

We visited with him briefly as the camera was set up. I
wanted to put him at ease by discussing my questions ahead
of time. I needn't have bothered; he had obviously
rehearsed his story and launched into it with little prompting.

"My name is Lotan Jack. I was working with the

Japanese people on Jaluit Island as a coffee maker* for the high ranking Japanese officer on a small atoll about eight miles from Jaluit, Japanese headquarters. During that time we hear the story about Amelia..." the old man struggled to find the correct word..."Earhar--Ear'arts from Japanese Navy Officer. They said she was, her plane was shot down between Jaluit and Mili. That is about 30 miles from Mili. One Japanese ship found her and they pick her up and they took her to Mili Atoll. From Mili they took her to Jaluit and after Jaluit to Kwajalein. Last time they take her to Saipan. The Japanese officer, he tell all the Marshallese not to talk about her--that there are secret words about her. That she was on a flight around the world, that she was spying at that time--for the American people."

We expressed our thanks to the old man and he gratefully accepted NIK's invitation to join him for a cold beer while we held a conference to assess Lotan Jack's addition to our store of knowledge. I would have to listen to a replay of the tape to confirm what he had said after "shot down, between Jaluit and Mili". *Shot* down really grabbed my attention. Mili was eventually a primary Japanese fighter base, but not in 1937. Did this discredit his entire story? Reluctantly I put the likeable old man's testimony down as shaky; it would have to be verified. I thought I knew where to look for verification. Mili Atoll had figured prominently in all the stories we were hearing. It was time for a visit with the ruling monarch of Mili, Queen Bosquet Diklan.

We took time out to be interviewed on the local radio station. Mike handled the bulk of the discussion, emphasizing that we were doing historical research. It was a most satisfactory interview and the announcer concluded with a plea for anyone having personal knowledge of the matter to contact us.

That night Mike planned to show his film *Deadly Fathoms* in the Lanai Club bar. I was apprehensive about the reaction this frank discussion of the atomic bomb tests

---

* Interpreted to mean a mess steward.

might evoke, but Mike carried it off quite well. I couldn't
detect any feeling of animosity. President Kabua and First
Secretary de Brum joined us at our table and were most
cordial. To our surprise, de Brum agreed to be interviewed
on tape. He had been reluctant, he said, because his
information was secondhand, but he was eager to help any
way he could. We were most pleased at the offer, even if it
might not prove highly productive. Tom's impression from
the airplane placed de Brum in a questionable status.

We discussed with Kabua and de Brum the possibility of
Amelia's plane having been shot down by Japanese fighter
planes. The Japanese *did* have aircraft aboard some of their
ships. They were designed to be used as reconnaissance
craft; could it be that some of them were armed?

The consensus was negative. Even if a light machine
gun had been mounted on the flimsy scout airplanes, they
still would have been slower than Amelia's Lockheed. It was
highly improbable that they could get near enough to use
their armament effectively. The two emphatically ruled out
land based planes. The persistent rumors continued to
plague me however. We parted with an agreement to meet
de Brum early the next morning for a taped interview. In
the meantime they promised to help Ben arrange for us to
visit with Queen Bosquet.

A trail was emerging. A crash site in the vicinity of Mili
Island; a pickup by either fishing boat or naval vessel;
transporting of the wrecked airplane to Jaluit. Ignoring all
previous rumors, we would assume the trail stopped there
for the time being. That it would reemerge, by means of
painstaking effort, I was confident. A Japanese role after
the crash was firming up with each interview. I was certain
the old Queen would fill in some vital parts tomorrow.

****

Extracts from the Journal of T. C. Brennan III

November 21:
   Read the Earhart book Dominic left for me.
Can't see much new or different in it. NEW

information consists of message supposedly found in bottle washed on shore near Bordeaux, France in 1938. The writer claims to have been a prisoner of the Japanese and in cell next to Earhart and Noonan. Don't know much about ocean currents but all the way around Africa to France! Doubtful. Some people mentioned who may be worth checking. Two priests on Saipan who showed much interest when Goerner did his research there in the '60s. Remember Mike's talk about anti-American sentiments being at all time high about then.

Skaggs mentions the mysterious "canister" Noonan is supposed to have buried on an island. That's in a couple of other books. This author claims to have dug up a piece of metal at a spot pointed out to him by a native. What would be in a metal canister worth burying? Something incriminating like a camera? Maybe worth asking about on Mili tomorrow.

This morning Mike, NIK and I went to other end of island to shoot some of the jungle footage Mike wants. First time I've been to extreme end. Jungle! It's like a solid wall. I remember Buddy's reassurance about no snakes. I just hope the snakes know as much about that as Buddy does!

NIK and I do some diving in the lagoon later. Beautiful water but almost as much junk on bottom of lagoon as on land! Really looking forward to seeing Queen tomorrow. Dick tried to prepare me-- says she is a real character. Just don't let her bear hug you! And watch out for whatever she offers in the way of libation. What does a Queen do all day? Saw her brother today, the one through whom Ben will make appointment. His Royal Princeship was asleep on cot on back porch of Lanai Club. Wonder how much longer it will take to get all the info Majuro has to offer?

Chapter Twelve:

THE EVIDENCE MOUNTS

We discussed our situation over breakfast at the Island Hostess. Time was becoming a critical factor. Tom was on a tight schedule to return. Mike always had a deferred project crowding him and I, too, had some business matters waiting. Today's interviews would exhaust our time budget for Majuro. We seemed unable to alter this lazy pace. An entire day was required for only two 30-minute interviews!

Tom was in favor of proceeding to Jaluit. "Most of our sources are providing information about things they saw while living there," he argued. "It's the point at which our reliable information ends; the last place Earhart and Noonan were seen alive. It's the logical place to pick up the trail."

Mike tended to agree. "There's the matter of the airplane," he pointed out. "Dick made a convincing argument that the Japanese would want to closely examine that Lockheed. If it had been transported on a barge, as John Heinie stated, it wouldn't have been easy to cross a thousand miles or more of open ocean with the plane in tow. Jaluit was a sizable naval installation; there would have been machine shops on the island. It would have been far easier to fly the engineers to Jaluit than to haul the plane all the way back to the mainland *and* keep the incident under wraps the whole time. The Japanese were very good at keeping secrets, but if that *Electra* were on the island of Jaluit for any length of time, *someone* saw it, especially if the Japanese made any attempt to fly it. I think we should stay in the vicinity of the crash site myself."

I wasn't so sure. Everything they said made sense but we would kill two days just setting up there. We had no names to interview; it would mean going through the same process as on Majuro. The prime motivation for going to Jaluit would be to trace the airplane. Although I still wanted badly to find the *Electra's* location, we had agreed before the trip started that the fate of the two flyers was our first priority. All rumors, and to some extent the information we had validated, pointed to Saipan as a more likely location to search. There was just not time enough to do both. Faced with this dilemma, the others agreed that unless our interviews with de Brum and the Queen turned up new leads, we would proceed to Saipan.

We discussed our plans and progress with Oscar de Brum while the camera was being set up in his office. "I think you are probably right," he said. "Everything would seem to point to Saipan. It was Japanese headquarters for the entire mandated area. The facilities were all there for an in-depth interrogation, including airtight security. But do not expect your investigation to be easy. The people of Saipan experienced far more harsh treatment at the hands of the Japanese than did the Marshallese. The island was an economic target of Japan long before the specter of war entered the picture. Saipan was a major producer of sugar; as many as 30,000 Japanese civilians lived there at one time. Civil law enforcement agencies were totally dominated by the Japanese even in the early '30s. You can expect deeply rooted distrust of foreigners, even Americans, among the older residents. The Chamorros (natives indigenous to the western islands) are more modernized than the Kanakas of the Marshalls, but for good reason; they are also less inclined to expose themselves to possible retaliation.

"The people willing to talk about the Earhart affair have told their story many times. One writer, Willard Price, spoke to more than a hundred Saipanese in the mid-'60s who remembered seeing Noonan and Earhart. But none have ever spoken about the specific disposition of the two. Were they executed? Did they die natural deaths from disease? Were they removed from the island to another prison? You have your work cut out for you to get beyond conjecture. I can give you two names, people who will help you get started. David Sablan has an automobile agency there. Many of his family who remember the Japanese occupation are still living. Manuel Muña, a retired senator, will also be willing to assist you."

Seeing that the camera crew was ready he turned to telling us a bit about his personal background. The de Brum family had come to the islands from Portugal in the 1870s. With a German partner named Capella, they bought the island of Likiep from the tribal chieftain. They did a flourishing copra business until the islands fell under Japanese control. It was apparent de Brum could provide us with much local history. He told us a simple but convincing story.

"I remember distinctly when I was going to school on Jaluit Island, about the first grade. It would have been in 1937. My father came home one day and informed us that an American lady pilot had been captured and that she was being taken to the Japanese office and that people were not permitted to go close to her or come anywhere near where she was captured and taken to the office. He did not say whether he actually saw her but the information he passed on to the family I recall distinctly--an American lady had been captured and had been taken to the Japanese high command office in Jaluit. This was in 1937."

Once more, a brief story but one with an authentic ring to it. A man of unquestionable integrity repeating a story passed on by a father with equally impressive credentials. The little bits of hard information were growing--painfully slowly--but they were growing.

As we boarded the little charter plane for our next interview on Mili, I was feeling a solid glow of satisfaction. If the Queen could supply a few essential pieces of information, the trail from crash site to Jaluit was well substantiated. I went over the questions: Had her husband, the Japanese commander, ever mentioned the fate of the two American flyers? Did she actually witness the crash?

Were the two brought ashore at Mili? Were they rescued by a fishing vessel or a navy ship? Was the airplane badly damaged? Were there guns or fighter planes on the island that early? I was hoping that as a bonus, we could obtain the names of Japanese we could still locate. Information from any Japanese source was seemingly impossible.

As before, the entire island population appeared to be there to greet us. As we waited for Mike and NIK to unpack the camera gear, I tried to visit with some of our audience. The percentage of those speaking English was much lower than on Majuro, however, and I gave up. I turned to speculating on what these people thought about, what they did, what was important to them. Those overriding needs of the human race--physical security, shelter and food--appeared to be fulfilled. What of the other needs like a feeling of self esteem? What on earth was there to *do* here to develop a sense of gratification? A nearby mound of coconuts represented someone's effort. I knew from our first visit that thousands of dollars worth of scrap airplanes and other by-products of war lay within walking distance, untouched for almost 50 years. Did no one yearn, even secretly, for some of the comforts money can bring, for the power over others it provides? Ships could be in the harbor within days, eager to buy this stuff.

I gave up, shaking my head. This was truly the land of the lotus eaters, the simple life, not a place to spoil with civilization. Will these people survive after the rest of us destroy ourselves with our awesome toys? I didn't think so. As proven during past wars, the innocents are frequently the first victims.

Queen Bosquet received us in the island custom, out of doors. There was a most practical reason for this--even the Queen's elegant residence, constructed of concrete blocks with a thatched roof, could hardly accommodate the entire assemblage. She was seated cross-legged in the sand, a large mat woven of palm fibers spread in front of her. Her Royal Highness was a big woman that even a voluminous red dress with a tropical floral pattern could not conceal. She favored us with an aloof air of benign tolerance, accepting our expansive greeting as a fitting tribute to royalty.

A lean wiry man, in his 30s I judged, squatted beside her. He was introduced as the Mayor of Mili Mili. A third figure, resembling the mayor in appearance, squatted to the mayor's left. He wasn't introduced and didn't appear to be particularly interested in the meeting. He was carefully peeling paper thin shavings from a small block of wood. It was hard to ignore him, however, for the instrument he wielded so delicately at his task was a two-foot machete! Accustomed to a society where heads of state are always closely guarded in public, I wondered briefly if this stalwart individual comprised the "palace guard."

Instinct told me this interview was not going to be one of our stellar successes. We were using, at her insistence, the Queen's interpreter, a young man educated in the United States who had elected to return to his native island. That should have told me something. He was barely literate in English and, I think, from the way things turned out, in Marshallese as well.

I had taken my place, by default, on a patch of sand immediately behind the Queen to her left. I was beginning to hate these outdoor interviews; invariably a razor sharp sea shell or piece of coral lay in wait for me. I offered my opening question. Would the Queen tell us her recollection of the time Amelia Earhart was on this island, and, I added, Who was the Japanese commander of the island and what was her relationship to him?"

The translator, who had remained standing in deference to Her Majesty, began talking. The Queen's reply consisted of exactly seven monosyllables. They came back to me translated as "She forgets the name."

Okay, I had been trying to go too fast. "Ask her if she remembers any significant events that happened about 1937."

This prompted a complete dialogue between Queen and translator. The Queen's expression puckered into one of intense concentration. This effort produced two sentences but no translation.

I broke in. "Just ask her to tell you everything she

remembers."

While this question was being converted into a short story, I scanned the faces of our little audience--rapt attention on every face. Apparently Her Majesty commanded vast awe and respect among her subjects. Perhaps her memory just wasn't up to par today. Her recollection consisted of, "The plane crashed on the ocean side of Mili Mili."

Mike was making frantic motions that he was getting no sound from the translator, because he was standing completely out of position. I had to repeat what I thought he had said for the benefit of the record. This interview was really boggled, but I determined to make the best of it. "Ask her if the lady pilot was brought ashore here."

Translated reply: "She did not see her. She hear from other people. It was a long time ago."

I sat back to collect my thoughts. Just what was going on? The old Queen had been effusive to the point of being garrulous when we were last here. Was it the camera? I studied her closely. She sat totally without expression, a serene gaze contemplating the distant horizon. I decided it wasn't the camera, but I was baffled. "Had the Japanese fortified this island in 1937?" I continued. "Were there airplanes here; the fighter aircraft?"

Translated reply: "Yes there were."

"Ask her, please, how does she forget the name of the Japanese commander?"

There were three complete exchanges between the two this time, evoking the response, "No soldiers, just Japanese businessmen. No airplanes."

I didn't even attempt to straighten out those two contradictory replies. "Was the island bombed?" Now the translator was getting help from the audience. I'm not certain the Queen herself had an opportunity to reply.

I had to be satisfied with, "During the war."

I tried once more, "And she does not remember the name of the Japanese commander who was here?" I broke into their discussion to add, "The one who was here in 1937, the Japanese businessman."

That one set off a roundtable discussion. The mayor got into the act, the machete owner and several bystanders spoke up. The conversation seemed endless. Finally, without acknowledgement of the question at hand, the translator replied, "Yes, one bomb was dropped. In 1938."

People viewing our video tape for the first time usually break up laughing at the expression on my face at that reply. In an attempt to salvage *something* from this fiasco, I asked, "Let's proceed in time--'42, '43, '44--does she recall anything of that period?"

I sat back to wait. Everyone was helping now. Eventually came the reply, "She was not here then. The Queen went to Kwajalein and did not return until after the war."

My God, so she hadn't even been here! I decided to cut my losses and run. Her departure date from Mili was vague and I didn't pursue the matter; wasn't sure I wanted to know. Just as I was thanking the old matriarch for her help and terminating the session, one ray of hope emerged. The mayor's father had been on the island during the war; he would talk to us.

The daily rain shower was upon us as we trudged nearly two miles to locate the mayor's father. It was a waste of time; the old man did not recall any fortifications or airplanes on the island before the war. Period.

The others remained silent as we boarded the airplane and departed--very tactful of them as I was furious. Finally I asked no one in particular, "Does anyone understand what went wrong back there?"

Mike: "That translator was something else. We could have done better drawing pictures in the sand and using charades."

I began thinking aloud. "She understood at least some of the questions," I'd wager, "but she just turned off at the part about the Japanese commander. Do you suppose she's ashamed of having collaborated? Is she embarrassed that he abandoned her and went back to Japan? Or is the story about her being married to him just legend that evolved from rumors?"

Tom spoke. "One thing which occurs to me is that

maybe he's the reason she *is* Queen. In my reading on the islands I came across royal succession. It isn't automatic, like the eldest offspring custom in Europe. There used to be heavy fighting among male heirs to the throne to determine the next ruler. Perhaps her husband exerted his influence on her behalf. Or perhaps all the male heirs were off on another atoll hiding from the Japanese. One thing is certain--there haven't been many queens on these islands; all I could find reference to were kings. Anyway," (he couldn't resist a sly dig) "she wasn't even on the island, remember?"

I was too disgusted to respond as we prepared for landing. What I was considering now was a trip to Jaluit. I wanted badly to learn more about the "shot down" remark Lotan Jack had made. I wanted to believe his story but if he was wrong about that part, how much of the rest was factual? What irritated me most was that we had wasted one of our precious days.

Our spirits took an immediate rebound when we deplaned. Ben was there to meet us and his first words were "Bilamon Amaron has agreed to talk on camera!"

The abortive interview with the Queen forgotten, we rapidly laid plans to talk with Amaron first thing in the morning. By packing tonight we could still catch the bi-weekly flight to Guam after the tape session. We turned in early.

I have no idea why the old Japanese decided to submit to an interview. Ben didn't seem to know either. Knowing Ben's financial condition, I momentarily wondered if he had bent my strict edict about not offering money for information.

Where many orientals seem to get smaller with age, Amaron--obviously always tall for a Japanese--had grown in girth. I knew he must be nearly 70 years old but he looked 50. He was still an active businessman; a huge gold wrist watch and expensive-looking sport shirt bore testimony to his relative wealth. I knew about what to expect from having read versions of his story in other reports, but I wanted to see and hear for myself. We set up the camera and didn't waste time with preliminary chitchat.

"Mr. Amaron, going back to 1937, what can you tell us about the Amelia Earhart/Fred Noonan matter?"

"Well, I was then a trainee in the Japanese navy dispensary on Jaluit, and it was at that time I saw her on the ship. One day the Japanese on the base were surprised to learn that a man with a woman piloting the plane have crashed. Many don't believe it. About ten o'clock that day I went with one of the military doctors to the ship (conversation is unintelligible) where I saw (unintelligible) the man was decidedly shorter. The doctor examined them and said there was nothing very serious. He told me to go ahead and treat the man; he had a little small cut on the front of his face and his knee. It was nothing very serious; I put some tape on the wounds, that's all."

I couldn't help but feel elation. At last, face to face with a person who displayed total recall not only of seeing our quarry, but talking with them! I prompted him, "And then you left the ship?"

"About one hour later. It only took a few minutes to treat the two people but the doctor stayed to talk with some of the ship's officers. It was then I was surprised to see the airplane hanging at the back side of the ship. The left wing was broken."

"Was it off completely, or just hanging there?"

"No, no it was hanging there."

"I see. And you administered to the man's wounds on the leg and on the head?"

"Yes, I did. I cleaned the places (we call them lacerations) and bandaged them."

"You were not able to talk with them of course. You did not speak their language nor did they speak yours."

"No, I do not speak English at that time. But there was an officer on the ship, a Japanese lieutenant, who speak very good English so he interpret for us."

"Mr. Amaron, did you know who the woman was?"

"Well, I heard her name at the time. But Japanese they call it different sound, you know? They call her Amee'-la, Amee'-la, Amee'-la. So I don't know if she Amelia Earhart or, just well...."

"Do you know where she landed, or crash landed, or set her plane down?"

"We were told by an officer that the ship left Mili about four or five o'clock (unintelligible) on its way to Jaluit. They saw the plane in the water about five or six miles west of Mili atoll, so they stopped and picked up the people, and continued on their trip to Jaluit."

"Do you know what happened to them after you treated Fred Noonan's wounds?"

"Well the ship was supposed to go from Jaluit on to Kwajalein then to Truk and from there to Saipan and Japan. You see the ship was...." Amaron groped for the right words.

I prompted, "A seaplane tender? Its job was to pick up planes?"

"Well yes, the boat they used to pick up the planes and they hang on the--what do you call it--on the back, they hang over like" (he makes a figure like a hook with his arms).

I prompt again, "Booms? Davits?"

"Well yes. And the airplane was hanging there, off the back."

"I see. Was it a silver airplane with two engines?"

"Yes, two engines."

"Did you get off the boat?"

"Yes. We talk a little while, about where they come from, where they go and then we leave."

"Do you recall the name of the ship?

"No. I know from later that the ship *Kamoi* called at Jaluit during those times but I cannot say for sure that it was that ship."

"Mr. Amaron did you wear a uniform then?"

"No, civilian clothes."

"Why was that? You were a part of the Japanese military establishment, were you not?"

"Well, no. You see when the Japanese come to build the fuel tanks, they hire lots of Marshallese. At first I am hired as interpreter. Then they ask if I like to work in hospital. I am Japanese but I was born on Jaluit. I speak both languages."

"I see. So, in summary, you treated minor wounds on the man, but the woman was uninjured. You saw a damaged silver airplane hanging from the stern. Then you left and do not know anything further about what happened to the two Americans."

"Yes. That is correct."

So ended what was, potentially, our most valuable testimony thus far. Was it accurate? We would dissect and compare the pieces to other bits we had. If Amaron's testimony were a fabrication, we had to know.

With the confusion of departure the team had no time for discussion until we were underway. It was then that I posed the big question, "Well what do you think?"

Tom's response was immediate. "Buddy, that guy was a professional witness. He had that story rehearsed down to the last self-depreciatory gesture. I would sure hate to cross-examine him on the stand. I'll bet you couldn't shake that story with a bomb."

Mike took mild exception. "I don't think you can discredit what he told us for that reason alone, Tom. Being on camera can be scary if you haven't been through it before. Keeping people from rehearsing what they want to say is next to impossible. The thing I wondered about was the pickup. Amaron implied that the ship carrying Amelia just stumbled across the plane on a routine trip to Jaluit. Why would the *Koshu* be ordered to drop everything and rush out on a search mission? I'd like to see an unedited copy of the message traffic during those first two days.

"One thing that supports his story is that the airplane was on board. The only way that big Lockheed could have gotten there was to be picked up in deep water or (if it went down on a reef or a beach) loaded by a lighter, a crane and a lot of hard work. That ship would draw probably 20 feet of water and there were no deep water docks around Mili.

"No two ways about it. If the *Electra* were hanging off the stern, I believe him. Otherwise he made up the whole story, which refutes Mr. John Heinie's emotional little story about waving flags at a boat towing a barge with a silver airplane on it."

"Towed it back from Kwajalein." We all looked at the source of this comment with surprise--NIK. I had thought he was asleep. "Simple. The *Kamoi* captain doesn't really know what he has. Takes the thing on to Kwajalein, Navy headquarters, where the brass is now working overtime. Best place to tear down the thing and look at it is in the shops on Jaluit. They tow it back here. Heinie didn't have any idea what day of the month he saw it. Another thing-- Earhart and Noonan were barely scratched. If I had been making up that story I'd have had them at death's door with myself as the heroic lifesaver. Amaron was trying to keep the Japanese from looking like monsters or he would have made a big deal out of their injuries. I'd say find out what kind of shape they were in when they landed at Saipan. Other books don't mention they were exactly carried ashore." NIK turned his head and closed his eyes.

That's the way it ended--inconclusive. I was beginning to detest that word.

****

Extracts from the Journal of T.C. Brennan III

November 23:
Underway once more. Will spend the night at Guam then on to Saipan. Buddy optimistic that we will score there. I can't share his feeling of real progress. Interviews on Majuro pretty convincing. I believe they went down in the Marshalls. But don't think Japanese left any tracks as to what they did with them! Just can't believe Amaron's whole story-- too pat.

Few regrets leaving Majuro. Will never know if Kwajalein any better--on the ground a total of 20 minutes. Same story as Johnson--NOBODY gets off without orders. All U.S. operation and secret. What on earth goes on out here?

Brief stops at Ponape and Truk. No deplaning here either, but for different reason--outbreak of cholera. Near panic at the possibility it will spread back to Majuro. The state of their sanitary facilities would really make that a disaster!

Guam. I do believe we have reentered civilization! Modern, clean airport. Nice homes, clean paved streets, my idea of a tropical island. Guam Hilton a little bit of USA, more fancy in some respects. Woodwork in room is teak! Dining room has white table cloths, big menu and a wine list. Hot bath (any time of day) and a good meal makes big change.

Everything looks Americanized but see very few Americans. Japanese are everywhere. Appears that half of Japan is just married and on honeymoon here. Had a most interesting visit with a couple after dinner--on their way to New Zealand to retire. He has taught school on Saipan since WWII. Was most interested in our little search mission. Verifies that people on Saipan accept fact that Amelia and Noonan died there. Not a lot of interest after all these years. He had no leads but did go on at length about people.

*Suggested we locate a book written by a pair of psychologists in '40s. Title is **Chamorros and Carolinians of Saipan - Personality Studies**. Authors Alice Joseph and Veronica Murray. Book deals with socio-economic history and impact of WW II on native behavior. Inhabitants made up of Kanakas from Guam and Carolines and the native Chamorros, little integration of two. History somewhat more violent than Marshalls. Island potentially rich in agricultural resources (Japs grew lots of sugar cane) hence always being exploited by stronger nations. Completely dominated by Japanese by mid-'30s. American invasion in 1944 traumatic--first violence since Spaniards left. Civilians were not even aware a war was in progress! Ran to* *hills and hid in caves. Were told by Japanese that Americans fierce and eight feet tall, so they should attack by hacking at the American's feet with cane knives! Most did not believe because "Americans are Christians too."*

After war, people confused and frustrated. Typical reaction to anxiety-arousing situation is outward submission but with underlying inner resistance expressed by inability to remember, understand. They procrastinate on things likely to lead to punitive measures. Hostility never openly expressed. Well-developed system of defense against administrative change. Not accustomed to freedom of expression. Essential loyalty reserved for family.

Sounds like a complicated people! Question and answer sessions will have to be approached even more carefully than in Marshalls.

Chapter Thirteen:

THE SECOND EXPEDITION

Saipan--the entire island was visible as the big Continental DC-10 entered a lazy circling approach. Unlike the Marshall Islands, Saipan is broken up by rolling hills. The same lush tropical greenery predominates but there is also evidence of greater population density--roads, buildings and cultivated fields. In a part of the world where agricultural land is extremely scarce, it is easy to see why this little dot of real estate has been fiercely contested for centuries. A little tingle of anticipation ran through me. This was the place where Amelia Earhart and Fred Noonan reportedly were last seen alive, and I wondered if this island held the key to their mystery.

The airport was a confused cacophony of a dozen different tongues. Oriental and European faces, even a robed Arab blended with the distinctive Chamorro natives. The air of excitement and bustling activity differed greatly from the easy-going attitude in the Marshalls. Fortunately David Sablan was on hand to ease our way through the confusion. Mike Harris had known Sablan and had contacted him before we left Majuro. Wherever we went, Mike seemed to know the right people.

If I were to single out one factor most responsible for the success of our mission, it would be David Sablan. He devoted untold hours and days in our behalf. He opened doors, provided introductions to people who (largely due to his endorsement) would relate events they had kept secret for 40 years. His knowledge of local history, customs and politics was phenomenal.

Sablan is a handsome man. Slender, with a receding hairline, his even-featured face seems permanently creased in an amused, tolerant smile. He is a highly successful businessman, owner of Saipan's General Motors franchise and involved in numerous other business interests. One of these, to our joy, was the recently constructed Saipan Beach Hotel. Tom and NIK left immediately after lunch for a quick tour of the island. Mike and I retired to our room to discuss the schedule. David told us he had asked a friend who could help to join us for breakfast the next morning. Our quest was to provide the first of a number of startling discoveries.

Manuel Muña--Manny, as David introduced him--was of slightly heavier build than our host but with the same intelligent, outgoing air. His business card identified him as a retired senator. David had told him only that we were interested in hearing anything he could tell us about the disappearance of Earhart and Noonan. At first our conversation was general.

"I still carry a souvenir of your army," he mentioned good-naturedly. I encouraged him to explain. "When your troops came ashore in 1944, my family was terrified. I was quite small at the time but I remember that frantic escape to the caves north of here. Everyone had been warned by the Japanese that the Americans would rape and pillage the entire island if they landed. We stayed in the cave for days listening to the bombs fall and the big guns thunder. One day the shooting stopped, but the elder, who was leader of our group, cautioned us to remain inside. Soon we heard what one man said was an American voice, tell us we must all come outside.

"The elder was adamant. We would all be killed if we exposed ourselves. The voice warned us that the cave would be attacked if we did not surrender, but still the elder refused. The next thing I remember is an ear splitting explosion. The American soldier (I learned later that he was a Marine) had thrown a hand grenade inside our cave.

"The elder relented then and we filed outside. We were badly frightened I can tell you, or at least I was. There was much shooting still going on around the caves where some of the Japanese soldiers were still hiding. It wasn't until a soldier started putting a bandage on my leg that I realized I had been hit by a fragment from the grenade.

"The Marine who had thrown the grenade was very upset and tried to tell us something we couldn't understand. Later one of the men who spoke English told us the American had thought the cave held more Japanese soldiers. The Americans were far kinder to us than the Japanese and we made many friends. I'll never forget the chocolate bars they gave us.

"I have never understood exactly why, but that Marine gave us his gun. Perhaps it was to show he meant no harm or perhaps it was to permit us to defend ourselves from the few Japanese soldiers who had not surrendered. Perhaps he only intended it to be a souvenir; we could not talk with him. At any rate, that gun stayed in our family and the Marine kept in contact. He returned to the island only three weeks ago and those of us who remember the incident attended a dinner at which he was the honored guest.

"Yes," he patted his leg, "I remember your invasion well."

I felt the time was right to ask some questions. "Mr. Muña, we are attempting to trace Amelia Earhart and her navigator, Fred Noonan. Do you recall anything of that time?"

"No," (a slight smile) "that was well before my time, but there are many people who do remember seeing them here. The stories have been told many times to other American visitors."

"I know, Mr. Muña, but no one has ever discovered *exactly* what happened. Did they die here, in prison perhaps? Were they taken to the Japanese mainland? All accounts of the matter seem to end in nothing more than conjecture. They seem to have vanished here. The Japanese deny the incident, despite overwhelming evidence to the contrary. If we are to trace them, we must find some eyewitnesses here on Saipan."

Muña considered my words at length. Finally he responded, speaking slowly. "Mr. Brennan, you must realize that you are stirring up something we Saipanese have reason to forget. Almost every family on the island, David's and mine included, lost one or more members during the Japanese occupation. As a race, we survived centuries of occupation by doing nothing to invite punishment or reprisal. To come forward, even at this late date, and give public testimony with respect to Japanese atrocities is to invite such reprisal.

"Our people would cite three reasons for maintaining silence. You can observe now a major Japanese presence on the island. We have strong economic ties with Japan; we are not worldly people. Japan ruled here before--why not again, maybe even tomorrow? Should that happen, those who talked against the Japanese would suffer.

"During the war, many Saipanese accepted employment with a Japanese dominated local security force. They were responsible for punishing many of their countrymen. Perhaps we should have rounded them up after the war and held them accountable for their actions, but that is not our way, so a number of them live here today. There is an unspoken apprehension that, if provoked, these people would retaliate.

"The third reason is, ironically, an apprehensive view of Americans. For years, the American CIA carried out a secret operation on the north end of the island behind a security fence similiar to those erected by the Japanese. In the eyes of a simple person, any group conducting secret operations behind barbed wire is a group to be feared.

"To those of us who travel and follow world events, these fears seem groundless, but they do exist. You will find an abundance of testimony that 'yes, the two American flyers were brought here, were seen here.' Such talk harms no one. But to find an eyewitness, one who will point the finger, is another matter.

"To begin with, very few native residents would have been in a position to observe the treatment or eventual

disposition of two American prisoners. Japanese security
was extremely tight and the penalty for violation was
immediate execution. Garapan Prison, where Amelia Earhart and Fred Noonan were held, lay within one of the
maximum security areas. After the war started, in 1941,
native islanders were forbidden even to approach the place."

All of us listened with intense interest. Muña's explanation tallied precisely with what we had been told before.
Hearing it from one of the most highly regarded men on
the island, however, was sobering. Our prospects seemed
bleak. "But Mr. Muña," I protested, "you're speaking about
wartime security. The Earhart incident happened in 1937,
four years before war was declared. Surely things were
more relaxed then."

"Oh certainly. Until 1941 the Japanese employed many
local people inside their compounds, closely watched of
course, but yes, things were much easier then. However,
those employees had no reason to be highly observant. Most
of them probably had scant interest in activities at the
prison. I believe you will find people willing to talk about
those prewar times, but that is not the period you are
interested in."

"I beg your pardon?"

"No, the woman--Earhart--was still in prison in 1941.
Fred Noonan is believed to have been executed or died of ill
health before then. The disposition of Amelia Earhart did
not come until later, much later."

I was dumbfounded. Amelia *alive* during World War II,
four years or more after all accounts had pronounced her
dead?

I'm sure I stammered. "Mr. Muña, are you certain?"

"Reasonably so. Of course, as I mentioned, I was too
young to have any firsthand knowledge, but the story is in
my family. Even the tightest security has leaks."

Mike spoke up then. "Mr. Muña, do you know of anyone
who could give us an eyewitness account? How about these
Saipanese who worked for the Japanese as police officers?
You mentioned some still lived here."

"Native police did not enjoy the full confidence of the

kempeitai, Mr. Harris. None worked inside the maximum
security areas. It's possible they picked up gossip from the
Japanese but I seriously doubt that any would discuss the
subject. I can try to get an interview for you but I wouldn't
be optimistic about learning anything of value, especially if
you plan to use video tape.

"You might learn something from my sister, however.
She worked inside the prison compound for a time and did
laundry for the woman we believe was Amelia Earhart.
David has a sightseeing tour planned for you this morning.
While you are gone I will see if I can arrange for you to
meet my sister. Also, Mr. Harris, I will attempt to get you
an interview with one of the former policemen."

This was far more help than I had expected. I was
looking forward to a tour of the island but I resented
anything that might delay our fact finding. Nevertheless,
we agreed to meet him later and parted.

In spite of myself I was soon caught up by the beauty of
the island. Dave was a masterful guide and we became, for a
few hours, typical tourists. Signs of heavy fighting from our
invasion nearly 50 years ago are still visible. Two tanks
squat in water up to their turrets just offshore. Crumbling
concrete gun emplacements and the famous caves riddle
the north shore cliffs, the final redoubt of the Japanese--
their "Last Command Post." There are remnants of artillery
pieces fired until overheating split muzzle ends into petal
shaped curls.

Gazing seaward I could almost visualize the frantic
efforts to repel an inexorable approach of Admiral Marc
Mitscher's battle fleet. Finally, with defeat inevitable,
thousands of Japanese soldiers had thrown themselves off
the 90-foot "Bonzai Cliff" to escape the terrible indignity of
capture. This was a beautiful but somber place.

Our tour with Dave and lunch behind us, we rejoined
Manny Muña. He had arranged for us to talk with his sister,
Joaquine Cabrera that same afternoon. Although he knew
where one of the former policemen lived, he had been
unable to contact him. We would just have to drive to the
house and take our chances.

During the drive Manny provided a spellbinding account of his many experiences; he had been employed by our CIA for four years. He pointed out huge radio towers dominating the landscape. They were oriented toward Russia and Mainland China he explained, Asia's counterpart to Radio Free Europe. For years the northern end of the island had been reserved by the American government to train spies for infiltration into Southeast Asian countries. The trainees arrived and departed with blindfolds in place, to prevent them from disclosing, if captured, the American training site.

His story was interrupted by our arrival at the home of the former collaborator. The man was there, but refused even to open the door. For the first time we encountered hostility among the local people and were told to leave in no uncertain terms.

Somewhat shaken, we proceeded to Manny's sister's house. The old lady was enormously pleased to see her brother and treated us like royalty. Manny patiently led her through the time she worked at Garapan Prison for the Japanese. She did her best but 70 years had made an inevitable influence. At times her story was completely lucid; at others she would confuse what happened yesterday with events transpiring years ago. Still, she displayed an amazing memory where Earhart was concerned. Amelia had shown kindness toward Joaquine which had made an indelible impression. Her description of physical features was credible, but attempting to establish dates was futile.

The long trip was not without reward however. A lovely young girl, introduced as Joaquine's granddaughter Rosa, was an interested observer to our conversation. As we were leaving she mentioned a woman whom she believed could tell us more about Amelia Earhart. The woman lived just a bit further down the road. If we wished, she would see if the woman would talk with us. Naturally we agreed. It was from that casual, seemingly insignificant beginning that we were to make our major discovery.

Manny continued his saga during the drive back. I didn't believe he could surprise me further, bit I was wrong; the man was just getting started. He told us of a time when he was a ship's pilot, guiding ships through a tricky entrance to Tanapag harbor. During an assignment to a Japanese ship, the *Fukuun Maru*, a twin engine Beechcraft flew overhead as they eased the ship into the channel. It had distinctive twin rudders that made identity easy. The ship's captain remarked in an almost offhand manner, "That airplane looks like the spy plane I shot down many years ago."

When Manny expressed interest, the captain continued, "I was a young flight lieutenant at the time, assigned to the aircraft carrier *Akagi*. We were on a training cruise near the Marshall Islands. Suddenly we were called to battle stations and told that an American spy plane was attempting to photograph our installations. Shortly after, we were launched on a search mission and I saw an airplane which looked almost identical to that one. I reported this to the commander on board the *Akagi*. To my surprise I was told to force the plane down; to fire on it if necessary.

"The pilot ignored me as I flew by so I made my second run as a firing pass. I'm not certain I hit it but the plane went down and crash landed just off one of the atolls. We returned to the ship and I was never able to learn what finally happened. At a party one night, another officer confided to me that the plane I had forced down was flown by a woman. Her name was Amelia Earhart and she was supposed to have been on a flight around the world. I asked many times but could never learn more about the incident."

Mike leaped into this one while I was still recovering from shock. Two other sources who could not possibly be associated with a Japanese fighter pilot had used those words "shot down." I listened as Mike excitedly asked Manny, "Do you, by any chance, remember the name of that ship's captain?"

"No," Manny replied casually, "But it shouldn't be too hard to find. The *Fukuun Maru* belonged to Fujisawa Kisen K.K., the shipping firm. They should have records."

Mike was off and running. "Buddy, I'm going to call the head office of that Fujisawa Kissen outfit first thing

tomorrow morning. If that captain can be located I'll fly to
Japan and run him down. I can take a direct flight from
there back to LA and meet you."

I agreed at once. This would be a major development. It
would answer many questions regarding the Japanese
reluctance to cooperate. Manny Muña was proving to be a
gold mine of information.*

****

Extracts from the Journal of T. C. Brennan III

November 24:

*This is more like it! Saipan far cry from the
Marshalls. Modern rooms (shower works), excellent
food. Everything much cleaner and neater. Sablan
is a prince; he seems to know everything about
everybody and every happening on this island.
Muña is also a surprising person.*

*Trip around the place fascinating. Sugar cane
everywhere you look. More Japanese tourists than
on Guam if possible. Their economy must really be
booming. Funny people; they regard that Last
Command Post as a shrine. Place is full of prayer
boards three and four feet tall stuck in ground.
Inside they leave prayers for the dead, along with
blank rice paper and styli for replies. Many honey-
mooners; must be obligatory in Japan to take long
trips when you get married.*

*Bonzai and Suicide Cliffs scary places. Why
would military jump off one cliff and civilians the
other? Interesting story Manny told about civilian
suicides. Convinced that we were going to slaughter
everyone, they went by families. First they threw the*

---

*Once again, time was to rob us of a major information source. Mike did
identify the ship's captain. His name was Fujie Firmosa. His last known
address was in the city of Osaka. He was recently deceased however. Mike
decided to go to Japan anyway in an effort to locate any former pilots who
had served on the *Akagi* during 1937. As with all past and subsequent
efforts to obtain Japanese sources of information, this one was futile.

youngest baby over, then the next eldest, etc. Momma went after all the children, then the father ran backwards off the cliff so he couldn't see what lay below.

This place was really prepared for defense by the Japanese. At the Cabrera place this afternoon, wandered off the road just a few feet and found two machine gun bunkers--just crude pits with concrete poured around the top. Understand they are all around the coastline. NIK and I examined two American tanks off the beach that didn't make it ashore. Looked like they could be driven ashore after 50 years in the water. Amazing!

NIK has an ardent admirer! Rosa, the cute young woman we met at Manny's sister's house, is making a real play. Asked NIK to send her Elvis pictures and souvenirs. Not sure he knows how to handle it!!!

Filming trip tomorrow with Manny. Will do the cliffs and the prison and maybe the lady Rosa told us about, if we can locate her. For first time I'm beginning to believe Buddy is onto something. It all sounded so far-fetched at first, but after coming all the way here from Majuro and hearing stories that correspond exactly from people who couldn't possibly have collaborated....

Joaquine Cabrera, who knew of Earhart's presence on Saipan in 1944, is flanked by her husband and Mike Harris (right) and Brennan (left).

Garapan Prison - Earhart cell on far left

Main House, Garapan Prison

Garapan Prison

Earhart Cell

Chapter Fourteen:
A MOST STARTLING DISCOVERY

It was somewhat glum at breakfast. Despite our encouraging start, we were still coming up empty. The night before we had talked with more people but all had said pretty much the same thing--"Oh, yes; Earhart and Noonan came to Saipan. They were held in the town briefly then moved." Some said to prison, some said to Japan, some claimed they were killed or died of disease. They knew someone who had seen this or that and had told them. Nothing approached an eyewitness account. To add to our frustration, they were not particularly interested or concerned about what might have happened. Mike pointed out that after all, 50 years is a long time. I had to agree, grudgingly.

Our mood lifted with Manny's arrival, for he was always full of enthusiasm. This morning he was to show us Garapan Prison and other parts of the island. In spite of myself I was soon caught up in his running commentary. It is almost impossible for an American to comprehend what the inhabitants of this tiny dot of land have endured. Much of their turbulent past is due to the highly productive soil. Saipan has been a major producer of foodstuffs for centuries. At one time, it was said, all the flies in the Pacific migrated to the sugar mills here. Copra, once another important export, fell victim to a coconut beetle infestation during the Japanese occupation.

The islanders' experience with foreigners has never

been pleasant. Magellan shot seven natives for stealing one of his small boats during his stopover. English pirates bartered with the natives, then shot them. During the 1600s, a native revolt against Spanish missionaries was dealt with harshly; all but a handful of natives were relocated to Guam, their population declining almost overnight from about 100,000 to fewer than 4,000.

When the Chamorro natives returned in the late 1800s, it was to German domination. By that time the islanders had lost their once superior ocean navigation skills and their warlike tendencies. They became farmers. The Germans were harsh task masters, introducing forced labor. They forbade the production of a potent liquor, tuba, from fermented sap of the coconut palm.

The Japanese came and went next. Then Americanism was quick to catch on, old customs discarded. Women now wear slacks, the priests are more lenient, economic and social rivalry prevails. The so-called "new rich" challenge the old aristocracy. It is small wonder that confusion and anxiety are prevalent.

Our conversation terminated upon arrival at the old Garapan Prison. There is something chilling about buildings used solely for incarceration. Although this site was nestled in the fringe of an ever-enveloping undergrowth, it carried the brooding air of a medieval castle dungeon. It required little imagination to conjure up the suffering which had been endured behind these thick concrete walls. Old prisons are also extremely durable. This one looked as if it could be returned to use simply by replacing the infrequent wooden sections.

I turned and started toward a long low building to my right. Manny stopped me. "No that is the main building. Amelia Earhart and Fred Noonan were held in this smaller one over here." As we approached he continued, "This building contains only four cells. It was used by the Japanese as their maximum security facility."

I found the ancient rusted bars surprisingly sturdy, but I had to force myself to step across the crumbling threshold. This place gave me the creeps. I swear I could still detect that fusty odor of unwashed bodies, human excrement and stagnant air that seems to permeate even concrete walls. Only my extreme interest in what Manny was saying kept me from turning and leaving.

Manny was blithely unaware of the ghostly atmosphere, and continued, "In this cell was held a local man, Jesus Salas. He was a farmer serving a long sentence for stealing cattle, but he escaped in 1944 when the bombing started. I have talked with him. He told me that in this cell (Manny pointed to his right) was another local man but he did not remember his name. In this cell at the end was Fred Noonan, and at the other end, down here, was Amelia Earhart. They were separated to keep them from talking between interrogations, which took place almost every day."

Despite my aversion to this place I followed and looked inside. Immediately I wished I hadn't. Scaling concrete walls enclosed an area barely eight feet wide and ten feet long. The floor had long ago been claimed by tropical decay. Two tiny, barred, openings were the sole source of fresh air. The nightmarish layout was graced by one architectural feature which puzzled me. An open-topped concrete box roughly three feet square and possibly 18 inches high was situated in one corner. In response to my question Manny explained that it was the "sanitary facility." The thought of anyone spending six years in such surroundings was sickening.

Outside I questioned Manny further. "And this Salas remembers seeing Amelia in that cell as late as 1944?"

Manny gave a slight shrug. "Salas told many stories to many different people after his escape. Unfortunately he is no longer living to answer that question himself. She *was* seen here as late as 1941 however. My sister, among others, saw her when they worked in this area. After the war started, no one except Japanese were permitted inside the compound. It is said in my family she was here much longer."

"And Fred Noonan?"

Manny frowned. "I have never heard anyone say for certain what may have happened to him. He was injured when he arrived. It is possible that his injuries became badly infected, he may have contracted dysentery--many died of it, or he may have been beheaded in a fit of anger by a guard. Some say he caused trouble."

I turned and took my final look at that hell hole. Uppermost in my mind was something I had learned from talking to World War II and Korean War POWs. As long as you were certain that your whereabouts was known at home--through mail, Red Cross parcels and the like--things could be tolerated. Those held without acknowledgement, by the Chinese for example, went through a special kind of hell. They realized that loved ones had no idea if they were alive or dead, and it preyed on their minds. Amelia must have wondered daily if anyone had an inkling as to her fate. I shook my head and left. I was not going to come back, I told myself.

An interview with Rosa's contact who "could tell us something" was scheduled for the afternoon. Dave picked us up on his way to collect Rosa, who would act as our guide and interpreter. We followed a winding back road into the farming country. Lush growth, coming right up to the edge of the roadway, made it appear like we were in a long green tunnel. Finally we emerged into a clearing containing a modest farmhouse. It was there that we met Mrs. Nieves Cabrera Blas, a remarkable woman who told us a remarkable story.

Mrs. Blas' husband made a hasty departure after our introduction; he did not appear to be happy with our presence. Nieves, as we were soon to know her, was somewhat nervous with her foreign visitors but carried it off well. In minutes the entire team fell victim to her charm. Even Mike seemed in awe of her. It is difficult to explain her demeanor. Every movement reflected grace and self-assurance. In appearance she was Chamorran at its most elegant. Her light tan complexion was unlined despite nearly 70 years in the tropic sun. From her slightly built figure, she regarded us with an alert, benign expression. I was completely captivated.

Rosa translating, we started our discussion with general

questions about her family, her background and items designed to put her at ease. I was also probing subtly to evaluate her memory and powers of observation. I was amazed. Her answers were prompt, complete and concise without exception. At last we posed the key question. "Do you recall seeing the American lady flyer and the man Fred Noonan when they were here on the island?"

Her reply startled me. "Rosa says you are not from the CIA. Is that true?"

I recovered enough to assure her. "No, Mrs. Blas, we are not connected with the American government in any way. I am a businessman. Mr. Harris and my son are also businessmen. We are attempting to discover what happened to Mrs. Earhart for historical reasons." I could see that history held little interest for her and amended my statement. "You see her family does not know what actually happened. It is a very difficult thing for them, not knowing."

I had hit upon the right approach. She nodded; family ties obviously meant a great deal to her. Without further prompting she told the following story:

"During the time the Japanese were here, I lived with my family on a farm near the village of Garapan. A part of our farm lay next to the big fence the Japanese built to protect their base. It was necessary for us to go there to tend our fields. At first the guards paid little attention to us. But one day they tell us Japan is at war with the United States. From that time on our family had a special pass to enter the area. No other Saipanese were permitted.

"Before the war one day there is great excitement. It is said that the Japanese have captured two spy people. They are holding them in the town. Many of us go there to see the two spies. I saw them in the square where the Japanese police building was. The Japanese guards made them take off all the clothes, everything they had on their bodies." The old lady seemed embarrassed at this point and hurried on.

"It is then we can see that one of the spies is a woman. Both of them were wearing trousers and I had believed both were men. I had never known before a woman who wore

men's trousers. The man seemed to be hurt and had a
bandage on his head. The woman was wearing a watch, and
some rings and some kind of medal. They take these, then
put her back in the cells. We learn in the village the
woman's name is Amelia Earhart and she was a flyer and an
American spy."

At last I had an eyewitness placing Earhart and Noonan
on Saipan, a source never before contacted by anyone! I
pressed on eagerly. "And did you see her after that?"

"Not for many years. We hear from other people she is
in the little prison building but she was never brought
outside the fence again."

"You say not for many years?"

The old woman's pleasant expression hardened. She
talked at length to Rosa who also asked her some questions.
Finally Rosa started her translation. From her shocked
tones I felt it was the first time she had heard the story.
"After the war is going on for many years we are surprised
to be bombed by ships and airplanes. The Japanese tell us it
is the Americans. If they land here we will all be killed--for
us to go to the caves. Then one day I am working on the
farm and I see three Japanese motorcycles. Amelia Earhart
is in a little seat on the side of one motorcycle. She is
wearing handcuffs and she is blindfolded.

"I watch and they take her to this place where there is a
hole been dug. They make her kneel in front then they tear
the blindfold from her face and throw it into the hole. The
soldiers shoot her in the chest and she fall backwards into
the grave."

I sat there in that little farmhouse, in the midst of a
jungle of sugarcane, trying to comprehend the enormity of
what I was hearing. I glanced at the others. They appeared
to be as stupefied as I. Mrs. Blas faced us without
expression. Two large tears trickled down Rosa's cheeks.
Before I could voice the thousand and one questions
churning inside, the old lady continued, Rosa translating in
choked tones.

"I ran from that place so the soldiers do not see me.
Later, I go back to see if they bury her, and they had."

"Mrs. Blas," I had to clear my throat to continue. "Is it possible you could find that place, the place you saw Amelia killed, again?" I held my breath.

"Oh yes. It was underneath the biggest breadfruit tree on the whole island. I went there often to get the breadfruit. The Japanese, they take all food we grow on our farm so I go there for breadfruit to eat. It is my mark."

I still had trouble believing what I was hearing. "Rosa, ask her if she could go with us, now, we have a car outside, and show us that spot."

The old lady nodded without hesitation. We crowded into Dave's van and were soon on our way back to town. I resumed my questions. "Mrs. Blas, have you told anyone else about what you saw?"

This evoked a vigorous negative shaking of her head. Rosa translated. "She is afraid the CIA policemen will be mad if they know. She is told you are a good person. She tell you but policemen not to know."

I spent the remainder of the drive convincing them that no one would be mad at her. She had done a fine thing for Amelia's family. From Mrs. Blas' expression, I'm not sure she fully believed me. She made it clear that this knowledge had bothered her for years. Many stories that were told were not true and she was relieved to have told the truth to someone at last.

We were skirting the edge of town by now and Dave was asking directions. Soon we were paralleling a huge parking lot surrounded by a seven-foot security fence. Several pieces of heavy equipment, road building and maintenance machines, were parked inside. We slowed and stopped at Mrs. Blas' instruction. As I watched in confusion, she pointed to a spot just inside the wire fence. Through Rosa she told us that was the spot where she had witnessed the execution.

Mike and I looked at each other in dismay. Almost in unison we asked the obvious question. "But where is the breadfruit tree?"

Dave entered the conversation now, explaining that the tree had been cut down when the equipment compound was built. "But without the tree, how can she be absolutely certain this is the right spot?" I asked.

Mrs. Blas remained adamant. "When I saw them cutting the tree, I marked the place by other signs. This is the place I remember."

Baffled, I studied the crushed coral surface of the parking lot. "Inside the fence?" I asked no one in particular.

"Inside the fence," Dave confirmed.

"Okay, who owns that property, Dave? Whose permission will we need to dig there?"

"It's government property I'm sure. At least it's their equipment. Just who can give you permission to dig, it is hard to say. Shall we go inside the office and ask?"

Alarm bells went off in my head. The full implication of what we had stumbled onto was just beginning to sink in. "I don't think so Dave. Something tells me we are going to have to proceed very carefully from here on. Why don't we set up the camera and have Mrs. Blas record her story and we'll have it on tape. Then we best go back to the hotel and talk. This whole thing is mind boggling."

It was Tom's suggestion that we *not* be seen shooting movie film at this location. We moved to a nearby park and made a brief recording. The second telling was as compelling as the first. With surprising agility the elderly woman mimed the shooting scene, the guards firing, then Amelia toppling backwards into a make-believe grave. When we ran the tape later I heard a hushed voice in the background mutter "Jesus Christ!"--a very accurate summation of our collective reaction.

Mrs. Nieva Cabrera Blas, above with Joaquine Cabrera's granddaughter Rosa, who translated her testimony. Below, Mrs. Blas with grandson at location she identified as execution site.

Chapter Fifteen:
A TIME TO REGROUP

It was a silent crew that assembled in the living room of my suite late that afternoon. A spectacular sunset, visible through the big picture window, drew no comment. David had offered to drive Mrs. Blas and Rosa home. NIK was out trying to borrow or rent a VCR; I wanted to go over that tape again. My mind was still in a turmoil from what we had seen and heard this day.

Facing Mike and Tom, I opened the conversation. "Okay, we have less than one day to find out whether Amelia Earhart is buried out in that parking lot. You know what that means. Do we turn around and make a trip right back here, all on the word of one elderly woman we know very little about?"

Mike spoke. "Buddy, I know exactly how you feel. I've been this route before. I can tell you a story a crew member related when we were pretty sure we had located the *Titanic*. Same situation--what do we do now? We have to come back. The 'what ifs' would keep us awake forever. We come back and dig and we either find something or we don't. If we don't, we just quietly fold up and go home. If we *do*, the fun begins.

"First thing, though--how is our witness going to handle this? If the remains of Amelia Earhart are really underneath that parking lot, there will be news cameras all over this town. That means interviews, offers for exclusive stories, maybe even something like a coroner's inquiry. Mrs. Blas is going to be at the front and center. How is she going to react to all this? She is a lovely, gracious, sincere lady; but can she handle this situation or is she going to freeze up and hide? If she does, her credibility goes to zero. Are we ready to expose her to an experience that may well end up being a real nightmare for her?"

This was a sobering thought. "We can protect her from a lot of that," I offered. "Get her an attorney. Keep her name out of it until the last minute; use press releases. David can do a lot along those lines."

Mike shook his head. "To a point, but sooner or later they'll get to her. Right now she trusts us, she trusts Manny and Dave. If we hustle her it'll backfire."

"Mike, I resent the word 'hustle'. I would never be a party to hurting that woman. But this is history Mike! We *can't* just turn and walk away now. What about Amelia's family? They've lived with this uncertainty for 50 years. Don't they deserve a final resolution? Just where *is* our obligation?"

Tom spoke up then. "I agree we have a moral question to resolve. But your mentioning the family leads to a question of our legal position. What are we going to need to go out there and start throwing dirt? Bear in mind this is likely to be an extremely sensitive matter, Earhart being executed by the Japanese right here on this island. For one thing the local government is going to feel pressure both from the Japanese government and businessmen. They have made it plain that as far as they're concerned, the thing never happened. Do you think they're going to stand back and be exposed as liars without lifting a finger? True, we have clout here but so do the Japanese. For that matter how much backing can we expect from our own government? From what I've seen, our official position is not too much different than Japan's.

"The next logical step is an exhumation order. Do we have a basis to petition for one? I'll find out, but if one is required I'll bet it has to originate with Amelia's immediate family. Now this would probably not be the case if this were a murder investigation. Is that what we're saying? Was she murdered by the Japanese? If so, are we talking 'war crime?' Is the local prosecutor going to open a murder investigation after 50 years? So we come full circle. Mrs. Blas is going to go through hell as the accusing witness.

"But this is the cruelest joke of all. I think we have agreed among ourselves that Amelia Earhart was involved in a clandestine intelligence gathering mission. Consider this. If she was, if the Japanese obtained a confession to this effect, then they may have been within the law by convicting and executing her!"

This thing was getting completely out of hand. My objective had seemed so simple--a plane and crew had disappeared under questionable circumstances. No satisfactory explanation had ever surfaced. The only thing I had set out to do was establish what really happened. Now, here I was in a position to do just that and I was enmeshed in a snarl of legal and emotional complications. I made my decision now, a tough one.

"Like it or not, we've come too far to turn back. We just don't have that option. We will explain to Mrs. Blas in great detail what to expect, but I shall make it clear that the project is going forward. Tom, I'll ask you to check out the legal ramifications, but regardless of what you learn, I'm going to dig out there where that old breadfruit tree stood, even if it means slipping out there at midnight with an oil lantern and a spade. Now, NIK, if you'll get that VCR set up I have some questions."

Tom and Mike had slightly amused expressions but there were no arguments. The television screen came to life and we became immersed in reliving the drama of Mrs. Blas' testimony. I had NIK stop it at the point where Mrs. Blas was explaining how she had seen the guards take Amelia to the execution site.

"Exactly when do you think this happened?" I asked the team.

"Well," Mike replied, "it was in 1944. We really pinned her down on that aspect. It was very close to the time of our invasion. She was positive about that."

"I wonder. Think about it. Once that invasion started, there was no let up--continuous bombardment from our ships lying offshore, more bombing and strafing by aircraft. After the initial bombardment, Marines began coming ashore. Mrs. Blas tells us she was going about her business on their farm when she saw the execution in progress. Yet all of the natives, including Mrs. Blas, say they headed for the caves when the first shell exploded--an inconsistency. If the Japanese wanted to dispose of the evidence (Amelia) before they were caught with it, things would have happened differently.

"Everyone we've talked with, including Dave and Manny, have stories about the invasion, the bombing, the caves and such. What no one has mentioned is that there were *two* separate attacks carried out against Saipan."

I had to smile at the expressions of surprise. "You knew I spent almost a year reading up on this place?" I continued. "After we took the island of Truk in February 1944, Admiral Marc Mitscher made a strike here--no attempt to land troops, just a little friendly visit to leave some calling cards.

"Well, he caught the Japanese flatfooted. They were totally unprepared and they panicked. Martial law was declared. An urgent shipment of troops and material was requested. Troop reinforcements arrived but most of the material was on a ship, the *Sakito Maru*, which we promptly sunk.

"The invasion itself didn't happen until June. In the interim this must have been a hectic place. Word was filtering down even to the Japanese field troops that they were getting pushed back on all fronts. They were woefully unprepared to defend Saipan and must have been thinking hard about tying up loose ends, Amelia Earhart being one of them.

"It figures that she was executed sometime between February and June. The Japanese were nervous and frightened but they weren't under attack; they had breathing room. Mrs. Blas' family would still have been allowed to work the farm because food supplies were critical. The next time we talk with her I want to pinpoint that date she saw Amelia shot. If she insists it was during the June invasion, I'll have to wonder."

"Are you doubting her story Buddy?" This from Tom.

"Not in the least. But if we go to the mat on this, I want every detail nailed down."

NIK started the VCR again. Shortly Tom asked him to stop. "Right there it hit me as she was describing Noonan and Amelia when she first saw them. She said Amelia seemed uninjured but Noonan 'had a bandage on his head and seemed to be limping.' I've had reservations about Amaron's story but that little bit makes me feel much better about the guy."

I hadn't shared Tom's skepticism toward the Japanese corpsman's account but I was glad to hear his concession. We ran the rest of the tape and made a recap. It boiled down to one thing--we had to find something beneath the spot where that giant breadfruit tree had stood. Once more we were out of time, but a lot of preparatory work faced us before we could expect to open that gravesite--if the spot pointed out by Mrs. Blas was indeed a gravesite. The missing tree bothered me. It was asking a lot of a person of her age to have such a detailed memory.

The others had drifted back to their rooms to do preliminary packing for tomorrow's departure. We would have dinner with Dave and Manny tonight and lay plans for a return trip. It would be largely up to them to obtain whatever permission was required to dig in that parking lot. In the meantime I was going back for one more look. I had no idea what I was looking for but so much had happened that I needed time to collect my thoughts.

I parked the rental car on the side of the road and returned to the area Mrs. Blas had identified. It was just impossible to comprehend, that innocuous looking surface, monstrous pieces of earth-moving equipment passing over it daily. Could the objective of one of the most extensive searches in history be reposed just beneath that crushed coral? The mere thought sent a little chill up my spine.

My ruminations were interrupted by a gruff male voice. Deep in thought, I hadn't noticed the approaching figure until he spoke. "And might I be of some assistance to you sir?" The clipped British accent and ruddy complexion left little doubt as to the man's nationality. There was slight suspicion in his tone and expression.

Flustered by this sudden intrusion I stammered out the first story that came to mind. "I--uh--oh no. No, you see I was here in World War II. Back on a little visit, business trip actually, and wondered if I could find the spot where we had some real heavy action."

I must not have sounded very convincing. "Yes, I noticed you and your party here earlier. Couldn't help but wonder at your deep interest in our machinery. You in the construction business are you?"

I was getting in deeper. I had a sudden inspiration. "In a way, yes. You might say so. Tell me, do you work here?"

"In a manner of speaking. I'm the yard manager," came the dry response.

"Well great. Maybe you can help me. Were you by any chance manager when this lot was built? It looks fairly recent."

The man's suspicion was still evident. "As a matter of fact I was. Why do you ask?"

"You see I remember we were dug in close to a great big breadfruit tree. I think I'm close to the place but I don't see any trees. Did you have to remove any when you built the lot?"

I was afraid he wasn't going to answer. That sounded pretty thin, even to me. But eventually he came forth with a grudging, "Yes we did, now that you mention it, four or five I remember. One of them was a big one, biggest I recall seeing. You're close to the spot all right; you're virtually standing on it."

Somehow I managed to extricate myself from the situation and get out of there. The yard manager stood in place and watched me out of sight. He hadn't believed me, I felt sure, and must really be wondering what I was up to. If he only knew!

I related my little escapade to the others over dinner. It seemed to be a clincher and we parted with vows from Dave and Manny to start laying plans for our return. It was a sleepless night.

****

Extracts from the Journal of T. C. Brennan III

November 27:

On board Air Micronesia (aka Air Mike) bound for home. What a trip! No idea when we left Houston that we would be returning with a potential bombshell. Must confess my thinking changed. Have looked at the whole thing trying to find something I wouldn't want to go to court with. It hangs together. If Buddy finds something underneath that parking lot a number of things are going to change for a number of people! Sobering thought.

We want to talk of little else since Buddy came back with the story that yard manager told him. Not too many opportunities though. This must be kept under wraps. Going to be hard to do when we go asking the technical and legal questions that have to be answered before we go back.

Still chuckling over airline screw up on Guam. By now we have acquired twenty pieces of luggage. They wanted four hundred bucks in excess baggage charges!

Tomorrow means back to lawyer work. I can't see any way I can go on the next expedition...but someday I will.

LEFT: Buddy Brennan, Mike Harris and Mrs. Blas' grandson at dig site; ABOVE: Harris holding blindfold recovered from site; BELOW: The blindfold.

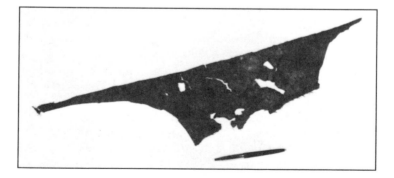

Chapter Sixteen:
THE THIRD EXPEDITION

Several months would pass before I could make all the arrangements for a return trip. The logistics seemed endless. We had a great deal of additional research to accomplish, and business demands kept eating into time I would rather have devoted to preparation. Tom was not available for this expedition, but Dick Huntoon would accompany us.

David Sablan had called me almost immediately upon our return with good news. Under local law we would be permitted to make an exploratory dig without a formal court order. It was at this point that I felt it appropriate to apprise Muriel Morrissey, Amelia's sister, of our plans.

Obtaining the information we needed without exposing our progress thus far was not an easy matter. Without benefit of soil samples, two professors of anthropology offered an informal opinion regarding the probable state of remains in a 50-year-old grave. They told me, in effect, that soil of volcanic and coral origin would probably be highly caustic and that I could expect an advanced state of decomposition.

Mike and I discussed the excavation at length. I planned to hire local labor to dig at the site by hand. We would personally examine each bit of earth removed. Mike estimated it might take two weeks to cover the area completely. It would be tedious work as any items we could expect to recover would be exceedingly small.

We retraced our steps to the exotic Marshall and

Mariana Islands, this time with an entirely different
outlook. Now there was a measure of trepidation in our
optimism. We told ourselves repeatedly not to expect too
much, possibly nothing, but my faith in Mrs. Blas wouldn't
allow me to think we might come away empty-handed.

I was impatient with the enforced layover on Majuro to
make our Air Micronesia connection, but it was not entirely
unproductive. I encountered a young man named Dwayne
Riggs who had been a PBY crew member after the war. His
plane had made regular runs between Kwajalein and
Tarawa. One day, for a break in the routine, they overflew
the island of Jaluit. Plainly visible just inside the break-
water at Jaluit was a twin-engine aircraft in relatively
shallow water. It was silver colored as opposed to the
wartime camouflage common to most of the hulks that
litter the islands. What might have been an exciting new
lead to the missing Lockheed *Electra* could not, unfortunately, be followed up at the time. I filed the information
for future investigation.

Dick Huntoon recalls the expedition:

When Buddy asked me to join his team for the
next adventure to Saipan, I dropped everything. I
wasn't going to miss this trip for the world! Still
open-mouthed at what he had brought back from
the last expedition, I was determined to be on hand
when that grave was opened. It was mind boggling.

Departure and travel arrangements were far
better than on the first trip, but somehow I missed
the excitement that comes with doing something
for the first time. Unlike the first adventure, my
fellow passengers on this flight seemed to be stoic
businessmen or busy people occupied with their
thoughts. The man in front of me sat swaying his
head from side to side or, for diversion, in circles,
obviously suffering a nervous disorder. I was sympathetic until the man's seatmate introduced himself as Mr. Lobe, leader of the Beach Boys. His

head swaying companion was their arranger, taking advantage of the long flight to do a little mental composition.

Then there was the kindly lady who sold me a stamp. Her face had struck a long-buried chord of recognition, and aware of my puzzled expression, she asked if I would care to dance to some "easy listening" music emanating from the P.A. It was then that the old memory clicked and I found myself dancing in the aisle, 35,000 feet over the Pacific Ocean, with Kathryn Murray. Her husband, Arthur, nodded approval from his seat.

I could immediately see changes when we landed at Majuro. Situated in a highly visible location was a modern Gibson Department Store. Ramen had been added to the menu at our regular restaurant. This Japanese concoction of dehydrated small noodles boiled in chicken broth, pork, beef or what-have-you promises to replace deep fried breadfruit chips, taro and coconut crab. It seemed to be a big hit with the Marshallese (and with me).

A restored freezer enabled the stocking of fresh steaks flown in from New Zealand, but I wasn't prepared for T-bone a la Marshalliase. The steak was two inches thick, covered the plate in approved Texas fashion, but was boiled! The most diplomatic rejoinder I could muster was to ask politely if I might cook my own--permission granted, thank Heaven.

Buddy discovered after arrival that one of his bags was missing. A radio call established that it had not made our last connection, but Air Micronesia was ever-efficient. The bag was safe and would be on the next plane to Majuro. Two problems--one, the bag had Buddy's medication; two, the next flight arrival was four days hence. A helpful airline representative steered Buddy to the local hospital where an emergency supply of medication was produced. On Majuro, however, all medical services are publicly funded. The patient is charged only the amount he/she can afford. Buddy was soon embroiled in such questions as "How much income did you derive from the sale of copra last year? How much from driving a taxicab? How much from the Marshall Island Security Program? How much from raising palm trees?" Somehow they ultimately agreed on a cash settlement of $7.50.

My first reaction was to blame the American government for converting these people to socialism. It seems, however, that the system derives from the Marshallese family-oriented culture--one takes care of one's brother. Grant Gordon, reporter for the Majuro weekly newspaper, explained it to us one evening. I had expressed curiosity as to how the taxi operators could pay for a vehicle costing them around $9,000 by charging 10-30 cents per trip. (A $5,000 Datsun in the U. S. costs $9,000 by the time it is delivered to the island.)

"Many are family financed," Grant explained. "Banks will not normally loan to a person with no income, so the man goes to a relative who is financially better off. Financing is invariably arranged if at all possible. Family influence is much stronger here than government regulation."

Despite our interest in the Marshallese, there was a feeling of urgency to get to Saipan. We were all on edge; what would we find in that area beneath the once-spreading giant breadfruit tree? Unfortunately, I was denied the opportunity to discover. An urgent personal matter demanded my immediate return to Houston and I said a reluctant good-bye to the team as they proceeded westward.

Along with fond memories, I retain two tangible treasures--a control stick salvaged from a Japanese Zero and a charm necklace. Although my wife had openly scoffed at the powers of that necklace, I reminded her recently that not once since my return had we been threatened by a lava flow or a disgruntled native warrior!

So I was to be without the able assistance of Dick Huntoon. It would be up to Mike Harris and me to complete the mission. After enjoyable conversations with President Kabua and First Secretary de Brum we proceeded to Saipan.

Settled into our comfortable suite at the Saipan Beach Hotel, we wasted no time getting an update from Dave and Manny. Dave had obtained permission for us to dig in the heavy equipment yard and would arrange to hire help. We would go to the office the next morning and complete the arrangements.

We spent the afternoon locating Rosa and renewing relations with Mrs. Blas. The poor lady was still very much concerned that she would get into trouble for talking with us. She feared the CIA might send her to the United States and put her in jail. We spent more than an hour reassuring her. It was during this conversation that we determined it had been after the bombing but before the invasion that she witnessed the execution.

Events did not go smoothly next morning. To preserve the integrity of our proposed dig site, Dave had not pinpointed the actual spot. Without his intervention, assuredly we would have been turned away. After the yard manager understood our purpose, he became most helpful-- until we showed him the area we proposed to rope off and spend two weeks excavating. That particular part of the yard, he explained, was a major traffic area. There was no way he could allow us to isolate it for that length of time. Even Dave's tactful persuasion was to no avail. The best we could elicit was a promise by the yard manager to "discuss the matter with the director."

We returned to the hotel to await a decision. I was furious. Had I come so far, with such high expectations on a matter of great historical significance only to be thwarted

by bureaucratic red tape? I made a rash renewal of my vow
to take a grave-robber's spade and oil lantern out there at
midnight, and an even more rash threat to buy the damned
lot if I had to!

Eventually the call came. I snatched the phone from its
cradle, holding my breath. The answer was "yes," but my
relief was short-lived. There was a condition--the entire
process would have to be completed on a Sunday, the only
day the yard was completely closed. Any excavation must be
filled and leveled by Monday morning.

I couldn't believe what I was hearing. I spluttered
protests. I explained the impossibility of completing our
work in one day. I invoked names of high officials I didn't
know. It was all a waste of breath. The reply (here phrased
more tactfully) was, "Do it Sunday or forget it." I sat down,
in a state of near shock. Our trip appeared to be a total
waste of time.

Mike was the first to recover. "Buddy, look. If we can
make an exploratory effort and find *anything* we can surely
obtain permission to make a more scientific undertaking.
Wouldn't you say so Dave?"

"I would certainly think so. Of course," he added wryly,
"I didn't expect to meet this much opposition. What damage
might we cause by doing a hasty job?"

"I'm not sure." Mike was frowning with concentration.
"We've been led to believe that any items surviving this
long will be difficult to isolate. We would have to keep the
opening quite small. Mrs. Blas is going to have to be very
precise in her location. I just don't know what to think." In
the end we decided there was no choice. The idea of
returning home without even making an attempt was
unthinkable.

Sunday morning found our little group assembled in the
office of the yard manager. Rosa and Mrs. Blas remained in
the van parked near the location to which she had returned
unerringly. With complete certainty she had pointed to
what she called "her mark." In spite of my impatience, it
was close to noon before we got underway.

The manager pointed out that almost two feet of fill had

been applied over what would have been the original surface elevation in 1944. He offered to loan us a front loader to speed up the preliminary excavating. We hired one of his operators and the great yellow machine roared to life, the moment of truth approaching rapidly.

Tension mounted. Layer by layer the coral surface was stripped away. Chunks of macadam surfaced. This evoked a muttered conversation between Rosa and Mrs. Blas. At my questioning look Rosa explained that the macadam was from the old roadway she remembered. I felt a brief wave of encouragement. I paced alongside the trench, hoping to see a sign of something foreign. Mike was evidencing strain as well. Mrs. Blas sat in the open door of the van, her face impassive. Rosa, I noticed with irritation, was doing her nails.

At Mike's shout, I wheeled in anticipation, but he was only signalling the front loader operator that he had gone far enough. I joined him as he gave instructions to the two young men we had employed to do hand digging. What we had now was a trench roughly four feet wide and about twelve feet long. At the yard manager's suggestion, we had laid a line between the giant breadfruit tree described by Mrs. Blas and the site of a second, somewhat smaller tree, the theory being that she could have confused the two.

Things became even more tense as the mound of loose black earth started to grow. The level of the excavation deepened with maddening slowness. I looked at my watch. It was after two o'clock and we had barely started, a depth of about two feet, then three feet. Mike and I were watching each shovelful like hawks. Nothing. "How deep would the guards have dug their impromptu grave?" I wondered. Mike muttered his frustration at not being able to put each bit of soil through sieves.

Three o'clock. I began to assess our odds of success. That gravesite could be as close as three feet from our dig site and remain as well hidden as if it were miles away! The front loader operator had been lounging in his seat, moving only to spit streams of beet red juice from the little nut he chewed as he worked. According to Manny these nuts contain a type of narcotic and are the native substitute for smoking pot. Now he offered an offhand observation that we should be striking the water table any time. Disappointment was growing bitter in my throat.

I was about to go to the van and question Mrs. Blas further, but I stopped in my tracks when I heard Mike shout, "Hold it! Let me see that." Mike was on his hands and knees examining something that was clearly not dirt. I wasted no time in scrambling down to join him. Together we started separating our find from the clinging damp soil. I noticed my hands were trembling ever so slightly and I felt foolish. Then I glanced at Mike's fingers and felt better; he was fumbling a bit himself.

We returned to the parking lot surface and examined our find, a scrap of cloth. Stained black and somewhat tattered, it had a definite shape but not one I could immediately identify. We handled the thing with extreme care. The object looked as if it might disintegrate at the slightest touch. Further gentle efforts proved the cloth to be surprisingly durable. We flattened it on a board and exchanged baffled looks. It was not a random scrap of torn cloth. It had been cut to a distinct pattern; portions of a stitched hem were faintly discernable. The top was cut straight and measured slightly over 24 inches in length. It was the bottom portion that puzzled us. The center segment was a uniform width of about six or eight inches, but on each side it had been cut in even arcs to form thin bands at the top.

I racked my brain trying to associate the shape with some article of clothing. It was fairly heavy cloth, tightly woven but not canvas or material used for bandaging. I could tell Mike was equally perplexed.

We looked up to find Rosa and Mrs. Blas. The two boys with shovels were also interested. Mrs. Blas was staring at the fragment of earth-stained fabric, a stricken expression on her face. She passed her hand across her face and muttered something to Rosa. The young girl turned to us and said, "She believes that is the blindfold Amelia was wearing. The soldiers removed it and threw it into the grave just before they shot her."

Once more we assembled in the Saipan Beach Hotel overlooking the water, just Mike, Dave and myself this time. The blindfold, spread across the coffee table, had a hypnotic effect. No one seemed able to speak. Finally someone mumbled, "Okay, do you believe it?"

"If it isn't a blindfold, what is it?" I asked. "Dave can you think of any type of clothing the natives wear, or used to wear maybe, that resembles this?"

Dave shook his head. "It isn't like anything I recall seeing."

"All right, accepting that it is a blindfold, wouldn't it have rotted away to nothing after being buried for 50 years?"

"Not necessarily," Mike opined. "Remember that the mummies they find after being buried for centuries are wrapped in cloth. The micro-organisms that destroy fabric may not be present in this soil. But if the blindfold survived, where is the rest of her clothing?"

"Mike, what we did today is like drilling for oil on 500 acres that someone tells you sits on top of an oil pool. We could have been within a foot of our artifacts. Until we get permission to cover at least a 10- or 15-square yard area we can't prove or disprove anything. But I believe we're close, very close. Be it a blindfold or something else, we found that piece of cloth 5-1/2 feet beneath the old surface. For the cloth to be that deep, someone had to dig a hole and place it there. Nothing casually discarded on the surface is going to work itself that far underground. We didn't find anything else to indicate it might have been an old landfill did we?*

"Something else occurred to me out there this afternoon. Those two big trees. When they were cut down, something had to be done to dispose of two good-sized stumps and root systems. If you have access to a lot full of earth-moving equipment, how are you going to remove

---

* We did find two other objects, thin glass ampules about 1-1/2 inches long. Their purpose remains unknown.

stumps? You're going to go in there and dig them out without worrying about disturbing a lot of the ground around them. Any fragments of remains could have been scattered in ten directions. No, I go back to Mrs. Blas' credibility. She hasn't shown the slightest hesitation in pinpointing the spot. I believe her. Manny and Dave believe her. She certainly has no reason to invent any of this! In fact, she is still terrified that the CIA is going to swoop down and carry her away. I believe we came within inches of finding human remains out there today. And I believe that when we do find them they will be those of Amelia Earhart."

A thoughtful silence followed. Mike spoke up. "Buddy, one thing she told us earlier comes back. She said something like, 'I left before the Japanese soldiers saw me. Later I came back to see if they had buried her, and they had.' It doesn't make much sense, but what if they didn't bury her there? What if they simply carried out the execution there and buried her somewhere else?"

"Why on earth would they do something like that?"

"I have no idea, Buddy." Mike shrugged. "The Japanese did a lot of strange things. Why did they blindfold her to bring her out there then take the damn thing off and throw it into the grave before shooting her?"

"I can offer an answer to that one, Mike. I picked up a bit of Japanese thinking while I was stationed in Tokyo during the Korean War. The entire Japanese military code of conduct was, still is to a certain extent, based on teachings of the *samurai* class warriors. This is quite different than occidental thinking, I assure you. According to the code, one's way of dying can validate one's entire life. For a warrior, no death is more odious than capture and execution by the enemy. It brings humiliation for himself, his family, his ancestors and future generations. Suicide is the honorable alternative. The manner of death is of utmost importance. Death by beheading is abhorrent. The act severs one's spirit from the hereafter. It is the ultimate statement of contempt for your enemy.

"Consider this. Amelia spent several years in captivity.

Contrary to popular belief, not all Japanese soldiers were complete ogres. Remember the Japanese guard that let John Heinie escape? Very often a bond is formed between captor and prisoner after protracted captivity, some type of syndrome. Let's assume the prison commander is not a fanatic practicing *samurai*. He sees invasion by the Americans and capture as inevitable. Suicide doesn't appeal to him, but he can see that having Amelia Earhart in captivity can get him hanged. He tells the prison guards, 'Dispose of the evidence.'

"Now put yourself in the position of the guard. You don't dislike the woman so you decide to not impose the supreme insult of beheading, the customary method of executing prisoners. You go even one step further and afford her the opportunity to face her executioners. If she does this without fear, she has 'validated her entire life.' I think it's plausible that they removed her blindfold as a measure of respect, if you can accept anything that bizarre."

Dave was nodding his head. "A strong possibility. I probably relate to the Japanese philosophy closer than an American and I can see it happening just that way. I agree with you. I believe Nieves Blas saw Amelia Earhart executed and buried exactly in the manner she describes. What is your next step?"

"Well, we simply must go back and finish the job. How do you suggest we get the appropriate permission?"

"I don't believe it will be all that difficult. We have Nieves' testimony and the blindfold to convince the authorities. It can't be done overnight, but I believe it can be done."

There it was. Another red tape delay. "Are you saying that we won't have time this trip?"

"Not unless you can stay for perhaps a month. I'm sorry, I really am, but you've spent enough time in the islands to know we move slowly in these matters."

God how I knew it! "But Dave, the site. Now that we've located it, everyone and his brother is going to be out there with a shovel!"

"I wouldn't worry too much about that. You've seen

yourself, there just isn't much interest in your project on the island; it's ancient history. Most could care less what's out there. Besides that, the British yard manager is on your side now. He's interested; he'll protect that site like a hawk, and it *is* inside his fence. No, I don't think anything will be disturbed."

I was disgusted and frustrated but I knew better than to try to force things. There was nothing to do but go back to Houston.

Mike did his best to cheer me up on the flight back. "Look Buddy. We've succeeded where the others failed! This is dynamite. I'm not sure you realize what you've accomplished. You're letting frustration get you down."

As I thought about it, I realized he was right. This time we were coming home with more to show than video tape.

Chapter Seventeen:
A TIME FOR REFLECTION

Shortly after returning, I held a press conference to report our discovery to the public. The response was gratifying, even overwhelming. I found myself talking to civic groups and dinner meetings in rapid succession. The mystique of Amelia Earhart is as alive today as it was 50 years ago.

There is one group, though, which has steadfastly refused even to consider the factual nature of matters. Our press release was provided to ten leading Japanese newspapers. Not a single word by them has appeared in print. The local Japanese consulate summed up their reaction. "We do not believe the Japanese people would do such a thing." Well they did. I have live testimony from eyewitnesses confirming that they did.

Another dissenting voice came from Fred Goerner, author of *The Search for Amelia Earhart*. Goerner supposedly remarked to a reporter regarding my announcement, "It appears Brennan may have taken a button and sewed a suit on it." I don't believe he intended the remark to be flattering but it gave me a chuckle. That's exactly what I did--the observation by old Tanaki, "They don't find it. It's still out there someplace," was the button. After five years of plodding research, building little fact on top of little fact, I had myself a suit.

Fate, that fickle lady was about to show her darker side, however. Plans for a return trip simply refused to jell. Mike had to withdraw; he was just overcommitted.

Efforts to validate the blindfold with respect to age and manufacturer developed into a real Catch-22 situation. The only forensic laboratories capable of authenticating our find seemed to be publicly funded crime labs devoted to supporting law enforcement agencies. I even contacted the Smithsonian Institute. What I got was a great deal of interest, encouragement and informal opinion. The cloth is made of cotton fiber, consistent with fabrics in general use during the early '40s. There is nothing to indicate it was woven more recently than fifty years ago. Yes, it could well have survived that length of time underground. But a formal, signed, official report would have to wait for the future.

Dick Huntoon joined me for our fourth expedition December, 1986. I had been in contact with Grant Gordon, the newspaperman on Majuro, to verify that we could dive on the "silver airplane" lying on the bottom of Jaluit lagoon. We enlisted the aid of two professional divers, David Olive and Mike Burnley, who would proceed from Majuro to Jaluit and examine the wreck while Dick and I went on to Saipan.

That was the plan. What happened bore no resemblance to the plan. Our first reversal came in the form of a late season typhoon which swept off the South China Sea and attacked Saipan with 193 M.P.H. winds. Upon landing at Majuro we were advised that a state of emergency existed on the entire island of Saipan. No one was permitted in except rescue workers. The state of emergency was predicted to last for at least two weeks.

Even our plan to proceed to Jaluit foundered. Our divers were placed on seventh standby for the little 22-passenger Dornier inter-island airplane. Defeated at every corner, we returned, dejected, to Houston.

There are still many loose ends. The inability to dive on that promising airplane sighting at Jaluit remains a bitter disappointment. The theory that Amelia may have been forced down by Japanese fighter planes dangles. Separate stories by persons who could not possibly have collaborated, coincide precisely. But without a determined effort by the Japanese government to locate crew members of the *Akagi* (some *must* still survive) or to produce a complete log of that ship's movements, I see no way to resolve that question. My recent requests to several Japanese newspapers to run a press release or paid advertising with regard to the Earhart incident remain unacknowledged.

Although our emphasis may appear to have been on Earhart, our concentrated search efforts were not at the exclusion of Fred Noonan. After reaching Saipan the two were separated and, being male, he did not arouse the same degree of curiosity among islanders as did the "lady pilot." Apparently other American male prisoners were held occasionally at Garapan. We did include Noonan in our research efforts; we were just unable to locate any eyewitness accounts.

The spy theory. Was she or wasn't she? While seeking additional intelligence files concerning Amelia Earhart, I had occasion to visit with a senior archivist for the United States Navy who was kind enough to offer some off-the-record opinions. He opined that such records in possession of the Navy have been examined many times over. I was welcome to return, he said, and conduct a personal search but he believed the microfilm copies I had obtained earlier were complete. I asked him what he personally believed happened that morning of July 2, 1937. His reply: "I believe she ran out of gas and crashed at sea. There is nothing in the official files to indicate differently."

I couldn't argue with that. "If she had been enlisted by President Roosevelt to gather intelligence, would there be any indication in existing official records?" I asked.

"Probably not." His reply pretty well closed that avenue. But I have not forgotten Joe Gervais' conviction that a "sacrosanct" file still exists. The spy theory remains a very real possibility.

Disturbing as they may be, these unresolved questions do not detract from the central issue: What happened to Amelia Earhart Putnam? We have eyewitness accounts (Carl Heinie and Bilamon Amaron) which place Earhart and

the airplane on the island of Jaluit at a time coinciding with
their disappearance. The records of the extensive search
effort imply, by exception, that the plane went down
outside the prime search area. People of unquestioned
integrity--the President of the Republic of the Marshall
Islands, his First Secretary, a practicing attorney, a Federal
Judge--all accept the fact that the plane crashed in the
Marshall Island group.

On to Saipan. That Earhart and Noonan were incar-
cerated in Garapan Prison is no longer open to speculation.
They *were* there. People like David Sablan, a highly
respected businessman, and Manny Muña, an ex-senator, as
well as members of their families remember the appearance
of Amelia Earhart and Fred Noonan on Saipan. The
shocking revelation provided by Nieves Blas is made
credible not only by her appearance and demeanor, but by
her ability to pinpoint the site of Amelia's execution. I will
never forget that hushed, shocked "Jesus Christ" heard off-
camera as she acted out the last moments of Amelia's life.

The blindfold removed by Earhart's executioners at the
last moment tells a story in itself. I defy anyone to regard
that soiled, tattered scrap of fabric without experiencing an
eerie sense of ancient tragedy. Authentication is still a top
priority.

I am frequently asked, "Are you going back?" A return
trip becomes increasingly difficult, but there is a need to
return. The fate of that Lockheed *Electra* still intrigues me;
I believe it can be located. An even more compelling reason
is to bring a tangible bit of evidence to Amelia's surviving
family. They deserve to have put to rest the uncertainty
and speculation they have harbored for a half-century now.
Beyond these reasons is, of course, the compelling urge to
bring this 50-year mystery to a final solution.

APPENDIX A

True Copy of Report From *U.S.S. Lexington*

[Author's note: Appendix B through Appendix E are supportive to the summary and have been withdrawn as redundant.]

Lexington Group,
U.S.S. Lexington, Flagship
Enroute Hawaiian Area
20 July, 1937

From: Commander Lexington Group.
To: The Commandant, Fourteenth Naval District.
Subject: Report of Earhart Search, forwarding.

Enclosures:
(A) Annex "A", Estimate and decision, Comdestron Two.
(B) Annex "B", Narrative of Search, Lexington Group.
(C) Annex "C", Aerological Data.
(D) Annex "D", Lexington Report of Earhart Search Operations.
(E) Appendix "A", Chart Photostat - Earhart   Flight Information.
(F) Appendix "B", Chart Photostat - Tract Chart Earhart Search, U.S.S. Lexington and attached aircraft.
(G) Appendix "C", Chart Photostat - The Earhart Search (Showing tracks of all vessels participating).
(H) Appendix "D", Photostats - Search Plan #1, and #2.
(I) Appendix "E", Earhart Search Plotting Sheet.

    1. Annexes and appendices are submitted herewith as forming as complete a report as possible on operations of the Lexington group, consisting of Lexington with Aircraft Squadrons VS-2, VS-3, VS-4, VS-41, VT-2 and VB-4 embarked, of Commander Destroyer Division Three in Dray-

ton, and Lamson and Cushing, during the period 4 to 18 July, 1937, inclusive, and of search operations of the U.S.S. Swan and U.S.C.G. Itasca while serving under Commander, Lexington Group during the period 11 - 16 July, 1937.

2. An effort has been made to confine the substance of this report to matters of fact rather than opinion.

3. Track chart tracings are being forwarded under separate cover.

4. The performance of duty by all units concerned was excellent.

The expeditious and efficient services rendered by the Fourteenth Naval District, the Fleet Air Base, Commander Minocraft, and Commander Submarine Squadron Six in preparation for the search operations, are greatly appreciated.

J. S. Dowell

ESTIMATE AND DECISIONS
EARHART SEARCH

I. MISSION:

To make the most effective search possible in order to locate Earhart Plane, or rubber boat, and personnel.

II. INFORMATION:

NOTE: All times used herein are Greenwich Civil.

A. KNOWN FACTS:

1. That Standard Lockheed Electra low wing land monoplane, No. X-16020, took off from Lae, New Guinea, latitude 146 - 55 E, longitude 6 - 45 S at 0000 GCT 2 July, 1937, bound for Howland Island, latitude 0 - 50 N, longitude 176 - 41 W. Pilot: Amelia Earhart Putnam; navigator: Fred Noonan, expecting to arrive in 18 hours.

2. That the plane's color was dural, with orange trim.

3. That a two man rubber life boat, life belts, flares and emergency water and rations were carried.

4. Rubber boat had a pair of oars and could be kept afloat by patching material and hand pump.

5. That the plane was equipped with radio capable of transmission and reception on 500 KCS, 3105 KCS, and 6210 KCS; assigned call letters "KHAQQ."

6. That the take-off from Lae was delayed awaiting a time tick and repairing broken fuel line.

7. That the plane was equipped with an orange box kite to be flown as distress signal, and by means of which an emergency antenna might be carried to a moderate height.

8. That the distance from Lae to Howland is 2227 nautical miles.

9. That the plane was filled with 1100 gallons of gasoline prior to departure.

10. That the plane's economical air speed was 130 knots.

11. That its range in still air at this speed, with optimum carburetor adjustment was 3120 nautical miles, or an endurance of 24 hours at 45.8 gallons per hour.

12. That the plane's range in still air at 53 gallons per hour for 20.5 hours was 2719 nautical miles. app. a.

13. That the distance covered at average ground speed 105 knots in 20.5 hours would be 2152 nautical miles.

14. That the distance covered at average ground speed 120 knots in 20.5 hours would be 2460 nautical miles.

15. That the plane's position at 0720 GCT was given as 04 - 33 S, 159 - 06 east, putting it on its course at 111 knots ground speed. This was the only complete position report received.

16. That the following weather forecast was received by the navigator prior departure Lae: "Lae to 165 E: winds ESE 12-15; 165 to 175 : ENE 18; 175 E to Howland: ENE 15 and squalls to be detoured.

17. That the following messages were received from the plane:
0720, to Lae: Position report lat. 04-33.5 S, long. 159-07 W.
1030 Nauru Island heard "A ship in sight ahead."
1418 Itasca began receiving incomplete messages on agreed schedules. No answers to questions put to Earhart. No positions given. No success in attempted radio bearings by Itasca, and no apparent success by Earhart.
1745 "200 miles out."

1816 "100 miles out. Coming up (fast)."
1912 "One-half hour fuel and no landfall (Position doubtful).
1928 "Circling trying to pick up island."
2013 Line of position 157-337" (no reference point given).
2025 "157-337 heading north and south."

18. That the Ontario was stationed in latitude 3 S, longitude 165 E.

19. That the SS Myrtlebank was in approximate latitude 1-40 S, longitude 166 - 45 E.

20. That the Itasca was stationed immediately to northeastward of Howland.

21. That morning of 2 July Itasca was laying a heavy smoke screen which hung for hours.

22. That the strength of radio signals in Itasca was greatest at 1928.

23. GCT sunrise, Howland, on 2 July was 1745.

24. That the plane would float with empty gas tanks, if undamaged.

25. That plane's normal radio power supply was so located that it could not have been used with plane on the water. app. a

26. Morning of 2 July visibility to south of Howland was excellent. Heavy clouds were about 20 miles northwest. Surface winds ENE 6, shifting ESE 16.

B. PROBABILITIES ARISING FROM RUMOR OR REASONABLE ASSUMPTION

1. That the plane was equipped with an emergency radio set that could be operated from battery power supply.

2. That the life saving equipment was stowed in the tail.

3. That the color of the lifeboat was yellow.

4. That the plane had one side door and no escape hatch in top.

5. That gasoline stowage was in tanks in the passenger compartment, and that gasoline was pumped by hand to two 50 gallon gravity tanks in the wings.

6. That the following summarized weather forecast, received at Lae, as the plane was taking off, and later

transmitted to the plane three times, was received: "Accurate forecast difficult account lack of reports: conditions average - no major storms; dangerous local rain squalls 300 miles east of Lae and scattered heavy showers remainder of route; winds ESE 25 to Ontario then E to ENE 20 to Howland."

7. That the following weather conditions were encountered in flight:

(a) Ontario ENE force 3 (0700 GCT) SE force 3 (1900 GCT).

(b) Howland Island (2300 GCT 1st (pre-start)

0	ENE	14	3000	ENE	24	6000	ENE	30
1000	ENE	18	4000	ENE	26	7000	ENE	30
2000	ENE	19	5000	ENE	30	8000	ENE	31

8. That the altitude at which the plane flew would have depended upon weather conditions and the desire to estimate drift or pick up a landfall, and cannot be judged.

9. That the navigator was competent and experienced.

10. That about 1030 the plane passed the Ontario giving a ground speed of 106 or the Myrtlebank giving a ground speed of 118 knots.

11. That at 1928 the plane passed closest to the Itasca and within 100 miles, after a run of 2050 to 2350 miles.

12. That at 53 gallons per hour the plane made 140 knots in still air.

13. That the plane landed on an uncharted reef or island, or on the water, within 300 miles of Howland.

14. That the plane would float with engines nearly submerged, with wings nearly submerged, with fuselage partly submerged, and with tail surfaces out of the water.

15. That the Itasca first reported to Howland by semaphore that plane was NW of island and had evidently missed it (*res gestae*).

C. CONDITIONS DETERMINED FROM SAILING DIRECTIONS OR EXPERIENCE:

1. That the prevailing winds are easterly, 10 knots.

2. That the average current in the area to north and west of Howland Island is northwest, 1/2 knot (experienced

by Lexington).

3. That the current in the vicinity of Baker Island is westerly, about 20 miles per day.

4. That the current in the southern Gilberts is southwesterly about 1-1/2 knots.

5. That the current in the middle Gilberts is westerly, about 2 knots.

6. That the current in the northern Gilberts is northwesterly, about 1-1/2 knots.

7. That about latitude 4 north is the boundary between the southern equatorial current, flowing westerly, and the counter-equatorial current, which begins to form near the Gilberts, flowing easterly.

8. That along this boundary there are apt to be circular currents and areas in which floating objects would accumulate.

9. That with the plane nearly submerged and tailing with the wind, the wind resistance would be small and the underwater drag great, so that the current effect would be great.

10. That the currents given by the sailing directions were compiled from data obtained largely by sailing mariners, and the wind effect, included in current estimates by all mariners, would hence be fully accounted for by this data.

11. That a rubber boat would be most greatly affected in its drift by the surface wind, regardless of water current.

12. That with a rubber boat, the chances of rowing across wind sufficiently to make land would be excellent for a boat starting 100 miles or more to the eastward of the Gilberts, provided navigation equipment was available.

D. POSSIBILITIES ARISING FROM RUMOR AND REPORTS:

1. On 3 July plane gave distress call and gave position 1.6 and 179, north or south and east or west unreported. Coast Guard San Francisco Headquarters give credibility to this report.

2. That the plane was down on water north of Howland

as indicated by radio test arranged through station KGMB.

3. On 3 July plane reported down 225 miles NNW Howland and said something about "Putnam--fly kite."

4. HMS Achilles on 3 July heard dashes made by transmitter other than Itasca's in response to request by Itasca for dashes.

5. Radio bearings, 4 July:
Mokapu 213 (very doubtful)
Wake 144 - 10 (doubtful, passes through Tutilla, Somoa.)
Howland 347 true (approximate)

6. Rock Springs, Wyoming, reported plane on a reef, south-east of Howland Island.

7. Extremely doubtful report "281 north Howland drifting northwest" whether miles or degrees, and whether plane with relation to Howland or vice versa not known (6 July).

8. Report from Melbourne signed "Kirkby" "Plane between Howland Samoa group ten hours west" (8 July).

9. Freitas of Yroka reported Mrs. Putnam's voice saying "Plane on reef 200 miles directly south of Howland, both okay, one wing broken" (8 July).

10. Mrs. Noonan stated Noonan would turn back if in doubt.

11. Additional reported positions: 176 and 10.6; 213 miles WNW; 173 W-5 S Island Jesus in vicinity, also island nameless on course further north 171W-3S (9 July).

12. George Palmer Putnam requested on 15 July search of 170 E, 0 9 north, evidently reasoned for 2 knots drift from Howland due west.

III. EARHART PLANE'S MISSION:
To land safely on Howland Island before exhaustion of fuel supply.

IV. COURSES OF ACTION OPEN TO EARHART PLANE:
A. ALTITUDE:

1. To fly close to the water in order to take advantage of reduced headwinds and to obtain frequent drift observations and correct course accordingly.

2. To fly at a moderate altitude, descending as necessary to sight station ships and landfalls.

3. To fly at high altitudes, correcting course by frequent celestial observations, to increase fuel economy.
(Number 3 is the most likely method.)

B. COURSE:

1. To correct course according to drift observations at low altitude.

2. To head to southward of course as far as longitude 165 E., then to head for objective in accordance with weather forecast received.

3. To deliberately over-correct to southward with the intention of running up a morning longitude line of position through the objective.

4. To deliberately over-correct to northward with the intention of running down a morning longitude line of position through the objective.

In view of the difficulty in sighting Howland toward the eastward in early morning, of which Noonan must have been well aware, it seems most probable that he took either the course of action specified in 3 or in 4 above. Of these the former had the advantage of bringing the plane close to the Phoenix group in case of early shortage of gas, but the disadvantage of winding up over the open sea if Howland was missed. The latter had the advantage of bringing the plane over the Phoenix group if Howland was missed, but the disadvantage of being over the open sea in case of premature gas shortage.

The following indications point to adoption of the former course:

1. The plane was evidently in position to obtain observations during the early morning.

2. Visibility to the southward was excellent and the Itasca's smoke plume could have been seen 40 miles or more, whereas heavy clouds lay to the northward.

3. The Itasca's first estimate of position was northwest.

C. SPEED:

1. To run at speed higher than the economical speed,

130 knots, in order to arrive expeditiously and reduce the chances of bad judgement induced by fatigue.

2. To run at the economical speed, 130 knots, to provide a maximum factor of safety.

3. To run below the economical speed in order not to approach the objective until well after sunrise.

Of these, the second is considered far the most probable. The plane evidently turned between 1900 and 1930 and at 110 knots these times would give runs of 2090 and 2145 nautical miles along the course - somewhat short of the objective.

V. MOST PROBABLE ACTION OF PLANE:

It is most probable that:

1. The plane cruised at economical speed at a moderate altitude laying course between Howland and the Phoenix Islands.

2. That navigational fixes were reasonably frequent but somewhat in error.

3. That radio bearings were inaccurate or impossible due to atmospherics and to the recognized inherent limitations of high frequency direction finders.

4. That the plane's gas supply was slightly diminished either by a leak or by non-economical adjustment of the carburetor.

5. That headwinds stronger than expected were experienced.

6. That about 1900, while somewhat short of its objective, the plane turned and headed northward on a line of position run forward from celestial observation about 1700, passing nearest Howland Island at 1928 after a 65 mile run, and, at about this time, began to circle looking for the island.

7. That at about 2000 the pilot announced the direction but not the reference point for a line of position she was running on, evidently believing it to run through the island, and began running north and south across this line near the point at which her navigator believed the island to be.

8. That at about 2030 the plane landed on the sea to the

northwest of Howland Island, within 120 miles of the Island.

VI. OTHER COURSES OF ACTION OF PLANE:
It is possible also that:

1. The plane flew beyond the Island.

2. The plane headed south past the Island.

3. The plane landed on a reef or island either charted or uncharted.

TOTAL REASONABLE AREA IN WHICH PLANE MIGHT BE:
Date: 2 July; Probable: 360,000 sq.mi.; Most Probable: 57,600 sq.mi.

Date: 13 July; Probable: 720,000 sq.mi.; Most Probable: 163,200 sq.mi.

Date: 18 July; Probable: 864,000 sq.mi.; Most Probable: 211,200 sq.mi.

VII. OWN LIMITATIONS:
1. Number limitations:

Available: Carrier Group, Swan and Itasca. (Colorado ordered detached immediately upon our arrival).

2. Fuel limitations:

Set by Navy Department. The Lexington is the controlling factor, as it was directed she should return to San Diego from search area without refueling. This necessarily limits her speed and that of the entire Earhart Search Group, as the plane guards Drayton, Lamson and Cushing and the Swan and Itasca will have to fuel from her if they do not practice strict fuel economy.

3. Area per day possible consistently under fuel limits:

(a) Carrier Group 28,000 square miles

(b) Itasca (assuming 10 mile front) 1320 sq. mi.

(c) Swan (assuming 10 mile front) 1000 square miles

4. Total number of days possible:

(a) Carrier Group 13th to 19th - seven (201,600 sq. mi)

(b) Itasca 11th to 17th - seven (9,240 sq. mi.)

(c) Swan 11th to 20th - ten (10,000 sq. mi.)

5. Total number of square miles under imposed limitations 220,840.

6. Weather limitations: Frequent squalls which reduce visibility and at times make carrier aircraft operations over-hazardous.

VIII. ASSUMPTIONS:

1. That the plane landed on water or on an uncharted reef within 120 miles of the most probable landing point, 23 miles northwest of Howland Island.

2. That, if on the water, the plane drifted between the limits northwest 3/4 knot and due west 1-1/2 knots.

IX. COURSES OF ACTION OPEN TO US:

1. To systematically search the most probable area in a westerly direction so as to overtake a drifting plane, and so fit our potential search area as to best cover this area, considering its southern sector as having been adequately covered by Colorado and her aircraft and by Itasca and Swan.

2. To cover the most probable area including its southern sector, considering earlier search to the southward ineffective, and thus necessarily sacrifice some of the northerly or westerly area.

3. To search to the best of our ability the widely separated and remote areas mentioned in many conflicting reports.

X. DECISION:

To make the most effective possible search with all available forces by:

1. Requesting that Colorado complete search to southeastward, including Phoenix group, prior 11 July, then fuel destroyers on 12 July.

2. Using Swan and Itasca for westward sweep, including thorough search of Gilbert group and maximum probable drift limit;

3. Using Lexington group to its maximum sustained capacity for an intensive search from east to west covering the above defined most probable area except the south-

eastern sector;

In order to locate the Earhart plane, or rubber boat, and personnel.

APPENDIX B
True Copy of Report From *U.S.C.G. Itasca*

TREASURY DEPARTMENT:
United States Coast Guard ITASCA
Honolulu, T. II.
29 July, 1937

From: Commanding Officer, ITASCA
To: Commandant, 14th Naval District, Pearl Harbor, T. H.

Subject: Earhart Flight.

1. The following report is submitted herewith for your information:

19 to 23 June, 1937:
Enroute to Howland Island. 2056, on 23rd raised Howland Island bearing 90 degrees true, distance 7 miles, stopped and drifted to the westward of the island awaiting daybreak.

24 June, 1937:
0718, closed island, stopped and drifted. Lowered boats and commenced landing stores and equipment together with gasoline and equipment for Earhart flight. Completed landing of stores and equipment at Howland Island this date and drifted during night on the lee side of the island.

25 June, 1937:
Proceeded to Baker Island where hove to at 0847 and commenced landing stores for that island which duty was completed at 1105.

26 to 30 June:
Holding position off and on leeside of Howland Island awaiting arrival of Amelia Earhart plane from Lae, New

Guinea. During this period Department of Interior personnel and technical aides at work on runways and precautionary efforts connected with Earhart flight. Organized task groups for landing and take off duties.

1 July, 1937:

1858, received verification from San Francisco Division that Amelia Earhart Putnam had departed Lae, New Guinea at noon, Lae time, and was enroute to Howland.

2 July, 1937:

Made preparation during night for landing task groups in connection with plane flight. Vessel in contact with Earhart plane at 0245 and intermittently thereafter. Early reception poor. At 0610 sent task group ashore to take stations for landing of plane.

0614 Earhart reported position 200 miles out of Howland. Commenced laying heavy smoke screen at daylight. 0645 Earhart plane reported position 100 miles out. 0742 plane reported apparently over the island and gas running low but no land fall. 0758, plane reported circling and requested transmission on 7500 kcs for bearings. 0800, plane reported reception of our signals but unable to obtain a minimum for bearing. 0845, plane reported as being on line 157-337 and running north and south, no reference point given, reception excellent. 0900, signalled shore party to return to ship as by this time fears were felt that the Earhart plane had probably landed wide of the island. Landing party returned at 0912.

As soon as the plane had indicated that it was still aloft at 0845 and possibly on a line which would provide a land fall it was deemed advisable to retain homing position at Howland with the vessel for some time on the possibility that the plane might still come in.

At 1040, it was definitely assumed that the plane was down so got underway at full speed and commenced the search in the area which at that time seemed most logical.

"FACTS"

(a) Flying conditions within a radius of 40 miles of Howland excellent, wind east 8 to 13 miles, ceiling unlimited, sea smooth.

(b)   Visibility south and east of Howland excellent and unlimited as far as could be observed. Sun rising clear and bright and island, ship and smoke screen in the glare thereof.

(c)   Visibility north and west of Howland excellent to horizon but beyond that continuous banks of heavy cumulus clouds.

(d)   Plane transmissions had indicated flight through cloudy and overcast skies throughout the night and morning.

(e)   Plane transmissions had indicated that dead reckoning distance had been accomplished.

(f)   Plane signal strength high and unchanged during the last hour of transmission.

(g)   Plane's line (of position?) indicated dead reckoning run correct.

(h)   Stellar navigating possibilities, south and east of Howland and close to Howland, were excellent throughout the night.

"ASSUMPTIONS"

(a)   That plane obtained no fix during latter part of flight due to visibility and assumed further this due to flying in cloudy weather and conditions which did not exist south and east of Howland but did exist north and west.

(b)   That line of position obtained was a "sun" line obtained when they emerged from the cloudy area north and west of Howland and presumably the only observation made during the latter part of the flight. Further assumed that this line was correct.

(c)   Assume that plane may have missed smoke screen, ship or island visually due to their lying in the glare of the rising sun.

(d)   Assumed further that plane passed within 200 miles of Howland Island and north of it.

(e)   Assumed that plane may have carried line of position found along line of flight for the period necessary for navigator to work and plot line of position not in excess of 100 miles.

(f)   Assume plane did not come down within a radius of 40 miles of Howland.

Upon foregoing facts and assumptions it was decided that the most logical area of search lay in a sector of a circle between 40 miles and 200 miles off of Howland Island and between bearings 337 and 45 true, from the island. Search was accordingly laid down in accordance with this estimate.

The following Department of Interior personnel were left on Howland in excess of normal personnel for the purpose of assisting the plane, if, by any chance, it neared the island during the absence of the Itasca:
Ah Kin Loong; Albert K. Akana, Jr.; William Tavares; Carl Kahalewai and Henry Lau.

Frank CIPRIANI, Radioman, second class, U.S.C.G.C, was left ashore in charge of high frequency radio direction apparatus to obtain bearings, if possible, on the plane. Searching throughout the day to the northward of Howland Island and during the night with searchlights. Extra lookouts posted and all hands on the alert. In addition to the efforts being made by the ITASCA, suggested to Commander, Hawaiian Section, the desirability of a Navy sea plane search from Pearl Harbor. Received information from the San Francisco Division that there was a possibility that the plane might use radio on the water and further that possibility of floating a considerable time excellent together with an emergency rubber boat and plenty of emergency rations carried.

At 2145 received definite instructions from Commandant, 14th Naval District, to be at Howland Island at daybreak Saturday, 3 July, 1937 to provide tender service for plane which had left Pearl Harbor at 1925. In view of the fact that the plane was already in the air enroute to Howland Island there was no alternative other than to abandon the search temporarily for the Earhart plane and proceed as indicated in the above noted orders; course was accordingly changed for Howland Island. Search was still maintained with searchlights.

3 July, 1937:

Arrived off Howland at 0710 in accordance with instructions. 0719 received information that Navy plane was turning back to base on account of extremely bad flying weather so resumed search to the northward which continued throughout the day. Received information from San Francisco Division that four separate radio stations at Los Angeles reported receiving Earhart position 178 with 1.6 in doubt. In view of possibilities of the plane being able to transmit on the water as indicated in prior information stood west to this latest reported position for the purpose of proving or disproving the reports which could not consistently be ignored. Maintained search throughout the day.

4 July, 1937:

Took up search during the 4th from 180th meridian towards Howland Island using rectangular search method and continued throughout the day and night.

5 July, 1937:

At 0242 received information from Hawaiian Section that Naval Radio Station Wailupe had intercepted the following message; "281 NORTH HOWLAND CALL KHAQQ BEYOND NORTH DONT HOLD WITH US MUCH LONGER ABOVE WATER SHUT OFF" With the possibility of plane transmission on the water still existing stood north towards the position indicated in the foregoing intercept and advised all steamers in the vicinity of the possibility of the plane being down at that point. Contacted Howland Island in a endeavor to obtain a bearing from that point on the reported plane and report from Howland gave a bearing which conformed to the report. Searched to the northward enroute to reported position of plane. Arrived about dusk broadcasting on plane frequencies and using searchlights intermittently for visual signals. At 2100 lights which had the appearance of flares were sighted to the northward and stood up to investigate. These reported lights had every indication of a bursting green rocket but were firmly determined to be attributed to meteorological shower which was reported both by the Howland Island

Station and U.S.S SWAN. At 2315 identified English steamer MORESBY who had diverted from her normal course to assist in the search. Continued search throughout the night.

6 July, 1937:

Proceeded south and east during the night to effect rendezvous with U.S.S. COLORADO on the morning of the 7th for fuel purposes. At 1445 received instructions to report for duty to the Commandant, 14th Naval District, and reported as indicated. At 1545 received instructions from Commandant, 14th Naval District to report to U.S.S. COLORADO for duty and conformed.

7 July, 1937:

Contacted U.S.S. COLORADO at 0445. Closed her at 0638 and 0705 commenced taking fuel by destroyer method. Received from COLORADO commissary stores as requested. While fueling Commanding Officer conferred with Commanding Officer COLORADO relative to search program and the general situation up to-date. 1010 completed fueling from the COLORADO, cast off and stood southward and westward for search area outlined in conference.

8 to 10 July, 1937:

Searched area south and west of Baker Island in accordance with orders of Commanding Officer U.S.S. COLORADO.

11 July, 1937:

0945 COMDESTRON TWO in charge of search. Continued search as indicated in original orders. 2224 received instructions from COMDESTRON TWO to proceed to ARORAI Island in the Gilbert Group and changing course accordingly.

12 July, 1937:

Proceeding toward ARORAI Island, Lower Gilberts, to investigate that island and others as indicated in orders.

13 July, 1937:

Raised ARORIA Island at 0600 and stood off shore to await further instructions from Naval command. Received final instructions to visit certain islands of the Gilbert group at 0700 and stood for ARORIA. 0835 stopped off ARORIA Island, native canoe came alongside with native Magistrate who came on board and conferred with Commanding Officer. 0850 landed two commissioned officers via native canoe with the permission and assistance of native Magistrate for the purpose of interrogating local inhabitants relative to the passage or wreckage of the Earhart plane. 1050 officers returned with negative reports on their efforts. 1402, underway proceeding to TAMMA Island. 1515 hove to off TAMMA Island. 1830 native canoe with native Magistrate came on board and departed with commissioned officers to interrogate local natives. 1714 duty officers returned with negative information. 1730, underway and stood to the northward and westward along the Gilbert chain.

14 July, 1937:

1322, stood inclose to lee side NADUKI Island but held no communication as no native boats came out and the surf breaking too heavily for surf boats unfamiliar with the locality. 1425, underway from NADUKI Island to intercept two native canoes sighted. 1452 stopped alongside of native canoe but were unable to obtain information due to their inability to speak English. 1510, set course for KURIA Island where arrived at 1610 under the reef and drifted. Lowered surfboat and contacted native Magistrate who stated that the islands of this group were in close communication and that no information was available concerning any plane or wreckage. 1710, underway to the northward and westward, instructions having been modified regarding particular islands to search and the reporting of this vessel at TARAWA Island, the Division Headquarters, being deemed essential.

15 July, 1937:

0650, raised TARAWA Island and stood in to westward

of reef. 0850, stopped and drifted off channel entrance. Dispatched Lieutenant Commander L. H. Baker and representative officers ashore in motor launch and motor surfboat to report the arrival of the ITASCA in the Gilberts officially and to explain the vessel's mission. At 1430 motor boats returned with following information: the senior commissioner received the party graciously but declined to receive the visit as official owing to the fact that he had received no prior notice of the vessel's arrival in the Gilbert group. He requested the ITASCA to notify the Resident Commissioner at Ocean Island which latter report was accomplished by COMDESTRON TWO. The Resident Commissioner at TARAWA Island stated that contact between the northern islands was close and that no information had been received of the passage of the Earhart plane or any wreckage therefrom. He further stated that a definite lookout had been kept for the plane at his instructions since the flight. 1455, with all boats secured, set course toward the southward at standard speed. Advised COMDESTRON TWO fully as regards the situation to-date and was directed to proceed to Howland Island for the purpose of picking up personnel and stores enroute to Honolulu.

16 July, 1937:

Enroute to Howland Island from the Gilberts. 1505, released from duty in search area by COMDESTRON TWO and reported to Commandant, 14th Naval District. 1725, relieved from further search duty by Commandant, 14th Naval District and reported to Commander, Hawaiian Section. 1740 received orders to proceed to Honolulu, T. H.

/ w k thompson /
W. K. THOMPSON
Commander, USCG

APPENDIX C
True Copies of Radio Messages

Extracted from official records of Navy and Coast Guard message traffic July 3, 1937 - July 5, 1937. Selected extracts reflect trying conditions under which search craft operated.

JULY 3, 1937

FROM: COMFRANDIV
TO: ITASCA COMHAWSEC

8003 FOLLOWING FOR WHAT IT MAY BE WORTH QUOTE FOLLOWING RECEIVED BY TELEPHONE FROM MCGILL AMATEUR STATION W6CHI OAKLAND CALIF QUOTE AT 0655 HEARD CALL SOS ON ABOUT 86 METERS AA POINT 225 NNW WEST OF HOWLAND ISLAND ASK PUTNAM AA TO FLY KITE UNQUOTE MCGILL TRYING CONTACT EARHART AND WILL FORWARD FURTHER INFORMATION AS RECEIVED UNQUOTE 1040

****

FROM: COMFRANDIV
TO: COMHAWSEC

8003 PUTNAM ASKS THAT EFFORT BE MADE TO CONFIRM THAT HMS ACHILLES GOT CALL LETTERS KHAQQ CLEARLY AND CERTAINLY 1030

****

FROM: COM12
TO: COM14

1703 PUTNAM REPORTS AMATEUR OPERATORS VICINITY LOS ANGELES HAVE INTERCEPTED POSITION

REPORTS EARHART PLANE ONE DEGREE 36 MIN-
UTES SOUTH LAT 179 DEGREES EAST LONGITUDE
PERIOD HE BELIEVES POSSIBILITY PLANE ON LAND
AND SENDING INTERMITTENT SIGNALS 1215
****

FROM: COMDT
TO: ITASCA (INFO: COMFRANSEC, COMHAWSEC)

6003 SECRETARY OF TREASURY MORGENTHAU DE-
SIRES LATEST INFORMATION CONCERNING SEARCH
FOR PLANE AMELIA EARHART PERIOD REQUEST
THIS INFORMATION BE SENT COASTGUARD HEAD-
QUARTERS IMMEDIATELY UPON RECEIPT OF THIS
MESSAGE 1756
****

FROM: COMFRANSEC
TO: ITASCA

8003 DUE TO CONFLICTING REPORTS OF RECEIPT
OF EARHART BROADCASTS REQUEST ITASCA NOT
REPEAT NOT USE 3105 OR 6210 KILOCYCLES NEXT
TWO NIGHTS TO PERMIT ABSOLUTE CHECK ON
AUTHENTICITY OF CALLS AND TO PERMIT MONI-
TORING OF ABOVE FREQUENCIES BY USE OF DIREC-
TIONAL ANTENNAE 1720
****

FROM: COMDT CG
TO: ITASCA

6002 SECRETARY TREASURY MORGENTHAU DESIRES
THAT YOU FURNISH THE LATEST INFORMATION
AVAILABLE ON EARHART PLANE AT TIME OF PREPA-
RATION OF A DISPATCH WHICH WILL REACH HEAD-
QUARTERS NOT LATER THAN 0630 PLUS FIVE TIME 4
JULY 1937 PERIOD ADVISE IF SIGNALS HAVE BEEN
HEARD AT ANY TIME AND IF SO WHEN THEY
STARTED AND WHEN THEY CEASED 2040
****

JULY 4, 1937

FROM: COMHAWSEC
TO: ITASCA

8004 RADIO OAHU PAA THIS OFFICE HEARD VOICE
CARRIER END KGMG BROADCAST 3105 CONTINUING
BROADCAST CONCENTRATING 3105 FOR REPLY SEV-
ERAL DASHES ALSO HEARD 0005
****

FROM: ITASCA
TO: COMHAWSEC

8004 YOUR 8004 0005 WE HAVE RECEIVED KGMB
CLEARLY ON WARDROOM RADIO AND CARRIER
WAVE 3105 KCS ON RADIOROOM RECEIVER BUT NO
DASHES PERIOD SUGGEST PAA CONCENTRATE ON
BEARING IF ONLY APPROXIMATE WILL COMMENCE
RECTANGULAR SEARCH EAST FROM ONE HUNDRED
AND EIGHTY BETWEEN ZERO AND TWO NORTH AT
DAYBREAK PERIOD THIS SEARCH WILL COVER AMA-
TEUR REPORTS 0020
****

FROM: COMFRANDIV
TO: ITASCA

8004 FOLLOWING FROM MONITOR QUOTE STRONG
CARRIER ON 6210 KCS BEING ON ABOUT FIFTEEN
MINUTES WE HAVE THREE RECEIVERS PICKING IT
UP MECHANICAL CHECK ON FACSIMILE PRINTER
SHOWS SIGNAL IS STRONGER FROM WESTERLY DI-
RECTION UNQUOTE 0400
****

FROM: RDO HONOLULU
TO: COLORADO, ITASCA

1704 FOLLOWING FROM MUTUAL WIRELESS WAHI-
AWA FOR WHAT IT MAY BE WORTH QUOTE MAN
NAMED DONALDSON WHO RESIDES WAHIAWA
PHONED HERE FROM 1200 GMT TO 1230 GMT THREE
OR FOUR CALLS HEARD MANS VOICE MAKE FIGURES

31.05 AND 31.07 SIGNED KHAQQ THEN LATER HEARD
62.05 THAT WAS BOTH HI FREQ AND INTERMEDIATE
ZENITH RADIO DIAL READINGS 171.2 AND 1200.4
THEN CHANGED SLIGHTLY SW READING CHANGED
TO 60.1 THEN TO 64.5 HEARD WORDS HELP UN-
QUOTE 0345

****

FROM: COMHAWSEC
TO: ITASCA

6004 FOLLOWING FROM MOKAPU PAA STATION AT
O445 TO 0500 ROUGH WEAK SIGNAL SPLITS BADLY
DOUBTFUL BEARING OF 213 ON GONIO MINIMA MAY
BE PLUS OR MINUS TEN DEGREES BAD SHIFTING
OFFERED ONLY AS POSSIBILITY 0540

****

FROM: COMFRANDIV
TO: ITASCA

8004 UNCONFIRMED REPORTS FROM ROCK SPRINGS
WYOMING STATE EARHART PLANE HEARD 1600 KCS
REPORTED POSITION ON A REEF SOUTHEAST OF
HOWLAND ISLAND THIS INFORMATION MAY BE
AUTHENTIC AS SIGNALS FROM MID PACIFIC AND
ORIENT OFTEN HEARD INLAND WHEN NOT
AUDIBLE ON COAST VERIFICATION FOLLOWS 1510

****

FROM: COMFRANDIV
TO: COMHAWSEC

8004 FROM PUTNAM QUOTE REQUEST KGMB
BROADCAST TO MISS EARHART THAT HELP IS ON
THE WAY AND THAT SIGNALS HAVE BEEN HEARD
UNQUOTE 1926

****

FROM: COMHAWSEC
TO: ITASCA

8004 BAKER ISLAND REPORTS HEARD FOLLOWING
NRUI FROM KHAQQ VOICE SHORT WHILE AGO HOW-

LAND HEARD WEAK VOICE 2240
****

JULY 5, 1937
FROM: CMDR SANFRANCISCO DIVN USCG
TO: COLORADO - ITASCA

8005 OPINION OF TECHNICAL AIDS HERE THAT
EARHART PLANE WILL BE FOUND ON ORIGINAL
LINE OF POSITION WHICH INDICATED POSITION
THRU HOWLAND ISLAND AND PHOENIX GROUP
PERIOD RADIO TECHNICIANS FAMILIAR WITH RADIO
EQUIPMENT ON PLANE ALL STATE THAT PLANE
RADIO COULD NOT FUNCTION NOW IF IN WATER
AND ONLY IF PLANE WAS ON LAND AND ABLE TO
OPERATE RIGHT MOTOR FOR POWER PERIOD NO
FEARS FELT FOR SAFETY OF PLANE ONWATER
PROVIDED TANKS HOLD AS LOCKHEED ENGINEERS
CALCULATE 5000 POUNDS POSITIVE BUOYANCE
WITH PLANE WEIGHT 8000 POUNDS 1535
****

FROM: COLORADO
TO: OPNAV

1005 PARAMOUNT NEWS NETWORK AND ASSOCI-
ATED PRESS SANFRANCISCO HAVE BEEN INFORMED
IN ANSWER TO QUERY RELATIVE PICTURES TAKEN
CONNECTION EARHART RESCUE THAT IF PICTURES
ARE TAKEN BY COLORADO THEY WILL BE RELEASED
BY NAVY DEPARTMENT WASHINGTON 1255
****

TO: COMFOURTEEN

HAVE TALKED TO CHIEF OF OPERATIONS RE EAR-
HART AND HAVE BEEN TOLD MAKE REQUEST TO
YOU FOR PERMISSION SEND PUTNAM NBC MAN AND
PARAMOUNT NEWSREEL MAN FROM HONOLULU TO
SCENE OF EARHART RESCUE VIA NAVY PATROL
PLANE PROVIDED YOU CAN PROVIDE SHIP STOP
PERSONNEL INVOLVED WOULD LEAVE SAN FRAN-

CISCO PANAMERICAN CLIPPER WEDNESDAY STOP
CHIEF OF OPERATIONS SAYS IF YOU RELAY OUR
REQUEST THEY WILL APPROVE PLEASE WIRE RUSH
IF YOU CAN SUPPLY SUCH TRANSPORTATION STOP
CHIEF OF OPERATIONS REQUESTS HAVE COPY
YOUR ANSWER TO THIS WIRE. CAREY NBC SAN
FRANCISCO

Copies of
Selected Documents
Relating to
Amelia Earhart's
Final Flight

GEORGE PALMER PUTNAM

OCT 19 1936 *38*

(SC) A 21-5

2 West 45th Street,
New York City.

October 16, 1936.

Hon. Secretary of the Navy,
Washington, D.C.

My dear Sir:

In accordance with conversations with
Admiral Cook, I am venturing this letter to place before
the Department certain matters in connection with the
round-the-world flight which will be attempted by my wife,
Amelia Earhart, probably early in 1937. The route contemplated is from San Francisco to Hawaii and thence
ultimately to the Rangoon-Allahabad established England-
Australia route. The course to be followed west from
Hawaii depends primarily upon what can be done in the way
of refueling, a matter which has been under discussion
with Admiral Cook.

Miss Earhart will be flying her new
Lockheed Electra plane. It is equipped with two standard
Wasp engines and has tankage for 1250 gals. capable of a
maximum cruising radius of about 4500 miles at minimum
speed. The plane is equipped with Sperry Gyro Pilot; the
best Western Electric two-way voice and code radio
communications; Bendix radio homing device. There is
special considerable reinforcement of the fuselage -- as,
for instance, all but two of the windows have been
eliminated thereby strengthening the hull.

Miss Earhart will be accompanied by a
competent navigator who, as it happens, is both a pilot
and a seaman, being now in command of a trans-Atlantic
passenger steamer, possessing a brilliant record of
accomplishment.

For your information, the plane carries
an NR license and is pronounced by the Department of
Commerce airworthy for the project in question, and has
been so recommended for the Department of State, which
courteously is cooperating in making the necessary arrangements for permissions, etc.

DOC. NO. 1162 C

Our desire is to avoid the hazard of the take-off at Honolulu with the full load. The full cargo of gas involves a considerable overloading. Further, to stretch out the gas-mileage to the maximum means very slow speed, which obviously adds to hazard by increasing the time over water, and likewise places a harder burden on the engines.

We would like to work out arrangements under which an aerial refueling operation can be conducted at Midway Island. The maximum of such refueling would be 500 gals. Possibly 400 would be enough.

Under such a plan the load for the Honolulu take-off would probably be kept at 1000 gals. This would bring the plane to Midway with about 700 gals. in the tank. An additional 500 gals. would bring it to approximate maximum capacity, supplying ample margin for the remaining 2800 miles to Tokio, or possibly a route via Guam to Manila.

The Lockheed Electra, as you know, is an extremely stable ship, and with its flaps is able to remain aloft under full control at a very low speed. Therefore, I am advised, it is a comparatively easy ship to contact and work with on a refueling operation.

Special top fuselage hatch and equipment leading to the tanks would of course be installed. Such installation will be made in close cooperation with such authority on the ground as you might designate.

In that connection I understand that the officer in charge of inspection for the Navy at the Consolidated plant in San Diego is experienced in refueling work. His guidance in this installation will be deeply appreciated.

Miss Earhart's plane will be stationed at Los Angeles after December 1st and would be available to have the above mentioned installation made at San Diego, the Lockheed plant at Burbank, or any designated point. It would be further available, together with Miss Earhart and the navigator, for some actual practise in refueling work at the convenience of the Navy in December and/or January.

It is our understanding that some new Navy boats now reaching completion in San Diego will after the first of the year be ferried out to Honolulu. An ideal situation of course would be created if one of these boats, with the crew that will man it at Honolulu, could undertake the refueling practise before departure from California. Thereby the two planes and the same crews will be used both in practise and in the actual refueling, so that the technique of operation will be mutually coordinated.

If between now and early December any technical points arise for discussion on the coast, Miss Earhart's technician, Paul Mantz, Union Air Terminal, Burbank, California, will be available for cooperation.

As a matter of general information, arrangements for the contemplated flight are being most painstakingly worked out. It may be stated safely that adequate preparation has been a feature of all of Miss Earhart's flying activities. Indeed, she herself often says that "seventy percent of the success of any expedition depends upon its preparations".

As a matter of interest I may add that the route westerly from Allahabad leads to Karachi, Aden, across Central Africa to Dakar, and then across the South Atlantic to Natal and thence the Pan American route northerly to New York.

In cooperation with an oil company having world-wide service, gasoline and appropriate spare parts will be spotted throughout the route and adequate mechanical assistance arranged at appropriate points.

It is especially requested that the entire project be held in strict confidence.

If the refuelling aid requested can be granted, the cooperation will be deeply appreciated by Miss Earhart and all who are associated with her plans.

Respectfully yours,

George Palmer Putnam

AMELIA EARHART

[handwritten note]

2 West 45th Street,
New York City.

November 10, 1936.

Dear Mr. President:

   Some time ago I told you and Mrs.
Roosevelt a little about my confidential plans
for a world flight. As perhaps you know, through
the cooperation of Purdue University I now have a
magnificient twin-motor, all-metal plane,
especially equipped for long distance flying.

   [handwritten: Mrs. Putnam and I]
For some months we have been pre-
paring for a flight which I hope to attempt probably in March. The route, compared with
previous flights, will be unique. It is east to
west, and approximates the equator. Roughly it
is from San Francisco to Honolulu; from Honolulu
to Tokio -- or Honolulu to Brisbane; the regular
Australia-England route as far west as Karachi;
from Karachi to Aden; Aden via Kartoon across
Central Africa to Dakar; Dakar to Natal, and
thence to New York on the regular Pan American
route.

   Special survey work and map
preparation is already under way on the less
familiar portion of the route as, for instance,
that in Africa.

   The chief problem is the jump westward from Honolulu. The distance thence to Tokio
is 3900 miles. I want to reduce as much as possible
the hazard of the take-off at Honolulu with the
excessive over-load. With that in view, I am
discussing with the Navy a possible refueling in
the air over Midway Island. If this can be
arranged, I need to take much less gas from Honolulu,
and with the Midway refueling will have ample

gasoline to reach Tokio.   As mine is a land
plane, the seaplane facilities at Wake, Guam, etc.
are useless.

This matter has been discussed in
detail by Mr. Putnam with Admiral Cook, who was
most interested and friendly. Subsequently a
detailed description of the project, and request
for this assistance, was prepared. It is now on
the desk of Admiral Standley, by whom it is being
considered.

Some new seaplanes are being completed at San Diego for the Navy. They will be
ferried in January or February to Honolulu. It
is my desire to practise actual refueling
operations in the air over San Diego with one of
these planes. That plane subsequently from
Honolulu would be available for the Midway
operation. I gather from Admiral Cook that
technically there are no extraordinary difficulties.
It is primarily a matter of policy and precedent.

In the past the Navy has been so
progressive in its pioneering, and so broad-minded
in what we might call its "public relations",
that I think a project such as this (even involving
a mere woman!) may appeal to Navy personnel. Its
successful attainment might, I think, win for the
Service further popular friendship.

I should add the matter of international permissions etc. is being handled very
helpfully by the State Department. The flight,
by the way, has no commercial implications. The
operation of my "flying laboratory" is under the
auspices of Purdue University. Like previous
flights, I am undertaking this one solely because
I want to, and because I feel that women now and
then have to do things to show what women can do.

Forgive the great length of this
letter. I am just leaving for the west on a

lecture tour and wanted to place my problem
before you.

Knowing your own enthusiasm for
voyaging, and your affectionate interest in
Navy matters, I am asking you to help me secure
Navy cooperation -- that is, if you think well
of the project. . If any information is wanted
as to purpose, plans, equipment, etc., Mr.
Putnam can meet anyone you designate any time
any where.

GSA, NARS
Franklin D. Roosevelt Library   Very sincerely yours,
Hyde Park, N. Y.

[signature]

Hon. Franklin D. Roosevelt,
The White House,
Washington, D.C.

P.S.- My plans are for the
moment entirely confidential
-- no announcement has been
made.

---

16 November, 1936

Memorandum:

For: The Chief of Naval Operations.

The attached letter was handed me this morning,
together with the information that the President
hoped the Navy would do what they could to cooperate
with Miss Amelia Earhart in her proposed flight and
that in this connection, contact should be made with
her husband, Mr. Putnam.

GSA, NARS
Franklin D. Roosevelt Library
Hyde Park, N. Y.

Paul Bastedo.

THE WHITE HOUSE
WASHINGTON

January 11, 1937

My dear Miss Earhart:

The President has requested me to reply to your tele-
gram of January 8, 1937 advising him that the plan arranged
by Admiral Standley to refuel your plane west of Hawaii on
the proposed round the world flight this spring has been
abandoned and that you intend to land, instead, on Howland
Island, if the construction of an emergency landing field
on that Island is completed by that time.

An allocation of Federal funds has been made by the
President to the Works Progress Administration to enable
the Bureau of Air Commerce to carry out the construction
of such a field.

I understand that the necessary equipment and labor
for this work will be transported to Howland Island by
the Coast Guard Service on a boat scheduled to leave
Honolulu on Tuesday, January 12, 1937.

Sincerely yours,

GSA, NARS
Franklin D. Roosevelt Library
Hyde Park, N. Y.

Assistant Secretary
to the President.

Miss Amelia Earhart
Union Air Terminal
Burbank, California

February 4, 1937

▬ Admiral William D. Leahy, U.S.N.
Chief of Naval Operations
Navy Department
Washington, D. C.

Dear Admiral Leahy:

If in order, I request the following assistance in connection with Miss Earhart's around the world flight.

1. U.S.S. Ontario to steam to a position about midway between Howland Island and Port Moresby, New Guiana.

   a. When Ontario is in position, Commanding Officer radio weather information upon request to the U.S.C.G. Duane at Howland.

2. Request temporary services of Lt. Arnold E. True, U.S.N., now stationed as aerologist at Fleet Air Base, Pearl Harbor, T. H., to accompany the March cruise of the Duane from Honolulu to Howland Island for aerological purposes and forecast for the flight between Honolulu and Port Moresby.

3. Request the Governor of American Samoa, Pago Pago, obtain collection of weather from Suva, Fiji, Australia, and other locations that will be helpful in the flight and transmit weather data upon request to Lt. True aboard the Duane at Howland.

4. Request a Naval aviation tender, such as the U.S.S. Swan now stationed at Pearl Harbor, to cruise to a position about midway between Honolulu and Howland Island to act as a standby ship in case of an emergency and transmit weather information as requested to Pearl Harbor Fleet Air Base and to the Duane. This ship to return to Pearl Harbor after Miss Earhart lands in Howland.

With the cooperation of Secretary Roper, Mr. W. T. Miller, Airways Superintendent of the Department of Commerce, is assisting in the arrangements for this flight. Prior to the flight, Mr. Miller will be stationed at Oakland in connection with his other duties. He will be in close contact with the Naval and other authorities. If agreeable, through him the approximate dates involved in the foregoing arrangements will be transmitted through designated channels.

Very truly yours,

J. P. Putnam

(Letter from LEAHY TO PUTNAM)   MAY 7 - 1937

My dear Mr. Putnam:

I am in receipt of your letter of the 4th instant, and wish to confirm your understanding that the Navy Department will be glad to cooperate with Miss Earhart's flight in a similar manner as before. This assistance will include the detail of the U.S.S. ONTARIO as station ship near the midway point of the Howland-New Guinea leg, a seaplane tender as station ship between Honolulu and Howland, two aviation ratings to proceed to Howland Island on the Coast Guard cutter assigned, and the services of an aerological officer. In regard to the latter, Lieutenant True, who functioned in this capacity during the last flight, states that, due to the limited radio facilities of the vessel assigned for the purpose, he considers that better aerological service can be rendered Miss Earhart if he remains at the Fleet Air Base, Pearl Harbor. The Navy Department proposes to adopt this plan unless otherwise advised by you.

Assuring you of this department's desire to assist in every way practicable, I am.

Sincerely yours,

Mr. George P. Putnam,
     2 West 45th Street,
          New York City.

CC: Bunav. Buair.
          Op-16. Op-38

W. D. LEAHY
Admiral, U.S.N.
Chief of Naval Operations

NAVAL MESSAGE

RECEIVED AT NAVY DEPARTMENT   44-3 (Enter) (204 445)

NPG 831

T BLOT V NPG NITE RADIO SANFRANCISCO CK 63 GOVT HYDRO SECOND

GOVT HYDRO ALL SHIPS AND STATIONS

US COASTGUARD SHIP ITASCA BELIEVES MISS AMELIA EARHART DOWN BETWEEN

THREE THREE SEVEN AND NINE ZERO DEGREES FROM HOWLAND ISLAND AND

WITHIN ONE HUNDRED MILES OF ISLAND POSSIBILITY PLANE MAY USE RADIO

ON EITHER 3105 6210 OR 500 KCS VOICE REQUEST ANY VESSEL THAT WHICH IN

VICINITY LISTEN FOR CALLS MADE CONTACT ITASCA CALL NRUI ON 500 KCS

HYDRO

HYDRO ACTION

2241 AC 2 JUL MX/

FORM 2451
TREASURY DEPARTMENT
U. S. Coast Guard
Ed. Sept. 1930

U. S. COAST GUARD

OFFICIAL DISPATCH

CRASH

DATE   2 JULY, 1937

INCOMING HEADING

UNIT HEADQUARTERS

FROM   ITASCA

TO (FOR ACTION)   SANFRANCISCO DIVISION

TO (FOR INFORMATION)
HAWAIIAN SECTION
12TH NAVDIST
14TH NAVDIST

ACKNOWLEDGE	PRIORITY	ROUTINE	NITE

ACKNOWLEDGE	PRIORITY	ROUTINE	NITE

TEXT

6002 EARHART UNREPORTED HOWLAND AT 1600 BELIEVE DOWN SHORTLY AFTER 0915 AM SEARCHING PROBABLE AREA AND WILL CONTINUE 1315.

MUSK KATY V TORT Z QUAC V BRUI QUAX P GR 83

FROM   CG ITASCA
ACTION   COMDR SANFRANCISCO DIV
INFO   COMDR HAWAIIAN SEC
PASSED TO OPNAV & COMTWELVE BY COM FOURTEEN FOR APPROPRIATE ACTION

6552 EARHART CONTACT 0742 REPORTED ONE HALF HOUR FUEL AND NO LAND FALL.

POSITION DOUBTFUL CONTACT 0645 REPORTED APPROXIMATELY ONE HUNDRED MILES

FROM ITASCA BUT NO RELATIVE BEARING PERIOD 0843 REPORTED LINE OF POSITION

157 DASH 337 BUT NO REFERENCE POINT PRESUME HOWLAND PERIOD ESTIMATE 1200

FOR MAXIMUM TIME ALOFT AND IF NONARRIVAL BY THAT TIME WILL COMMENCE

SEARCH NORTH WEST QUADRANT FROM HOWLAND AS MOST PROBABLY AREA PERIOD

SEA SMOOTH VISIBILITY NINE CIELING UNLIMITED PERIOD UNDERSTAND

SHE WILL FLOAT FOR LIMITED TIME 1015

RELAYED CG
FORED CAPT. TAFFINDER 1715

1759 AC 2 JUL MX/

FORED ADMIRAL RICHARDSON 1712
- BUAER D.O.   1715
- ADMIRAL LEAHY   1718 - INSTRUCTED NOT TO INFORM PRESS
- COMDR. ELDREDGE   1725

13   ACTION
05 10A 11   16   19 20 38
BUAER

NAVAL INTELLIGENCE
RECEIVED

JUL 3 1937

NPG 943

FROM: COMDR HAWAIIAN SECTION CG
ACTION: USCGC ITASCA
INFO: COMDR SANFRANCISCO DIV CG

8003. LAE NEW GUINEA REPORTS LAST CONTACT WITH EARHARTS PLANE BY

LAE RADIO WAS AT SEVENTEEN TWENTY FRIDAY GAVE HER POSITION AS 433

SOUTH 1597 EAST WHICH IS ABOUT 795 MILES DIRECTLY ON HER ROUTE

TO HOWLAND ISLAND 0030

13 ACTION
05 10A 11   76   19 38 20   BUAER CG/15
PX

0746 AP BY 3 JULY

JUL 3 1937

NPG 1124   S. K.

NUSK V KATY Z QUAC V QUAX P GR 100

85J UL 3 1 GT

0503 YOUR 0503 1555 REPLY TO INQUIRY FROM HAWAEC FOLLOWING FROM TUTUILA

QUOTE 1943 YOUR 0543 0925 REQUEST CONFIRMATION FROM HMS ACHILLES AND

FOLLOWING RECEIVED QUOTE AT 0600 SLANT3 GMT AN TELEPHONE TRANSMITTER WITH

HARSH NOTE WAS HEARD TO MAKE PLEASE GIVE US A FEW DASHES IF YOU GET US

PERIOD (50) A SECOND TRANSMITTER WAS THEN HEARD TO MAKE DASHES WITH NOTE

MUSICAL STRENGTH GOOD PERIOD FIRST TRANSMITTER THEN MADE KHAQQ TWICE

BEFORE FADING OUT PERIOD THE EVIDENCE EXISTS THAT EITHER TRANSMITTER

WAS THE AIRPLANE ITSELF PERIOD WAVE FREQUENCY WAS 3105 KCS SIGNED

COMMANDING OFFICER HMS ACHILLES UNQUOTE 1245 UNQUOTE 1433

2458 AC 3 JUL NX/

Post C

Form 9688
TREASURY DEPARTMENT
U. P. Coast Guard
Ed. Sept. 1936

U. S. COAST GUARD

OFFICIAL DISPATCH

DATE **4 JULY 1937**

UNIT HEADQUARTERS

INCOMING HEADING

CG4P1 Z QUAH V NRUI P GR 2Ø4

FROM
ITASCA

TO (FOR ACTION)

HEADQUARTERS

ACKNOWLEDGE	
PRIORITY	X
ROUTINE	
NITE	

TO (FOR INFORMATION)

ACKNOWLEDGE	
PRIORITY	
ROUTINE	
NITE	

TEXT

6ØØ3 YOUR 6ØØ3 2Ø4Ø FOR SECRETARY MORGANTHAU QUOTE NO INFORMATION
EARHART PLANE SINCE Ø843 2 JULY PERIOD HEARD FAINT SIGNALS BETWEEN
1825 AND 1658 2 JULY WHICH DEVELOPED AS NEARLY AS COULD BE ASCERTAINED
INTO CALL Q85 SIGNALS UNREADABLE AND FROM CALL LETTERS DEFINITELY
NOT EARHART PERIOD UNABLE CONTACT Q85 AFTER 1858 PERIOD WE ARE CALLING
EARHART FREQUENTLY AND CONSISTENTLY ON 31Ø5 KILOCYCLES AND UNDOUBTEDLY
AMATEUR AND OTHER STATIONS MISTAKE US FOR EARHART PLANE PERIOD WE ARE
PUSHING SEARCH AT TOP SPEED DAY AND NIGHT IN LOGICAL AREAS NORTH OF
HOWLAND AND HAVE THOROUGHLY SEARCHED 25ØØ SQUARE MILES DAYLIGHT ZERO
TODAY WITH NEGATIVE RESULTS PERIOD AMATEUR STATIONS REPORT UNVERIFIED
POSITION FROM EARHART PLANE WEST OF HOWLAND WHICH AREA WE WILL SEARCH
DURING DAYLIGHT TOMORROW PERIOD IF PARTY AFLOAT ON PLANE OR RAFT
THEY ARE DRIFTING NORTH AND WEST AT ESTIMATED MAXIMUM TWO MILES PER
HOUR PERIOD VISIBILITY AND GENERAL SEARCH CONDITIONS EXCELLENT
PERIOD SEA CONDITIONS TO PRESENT TIME NOW FAVORABLE IF PLANE OR
RAFT IS STILL AFLOAT PERIOD HAVE AUXILIARY RADIO LISTENING
STATIONS HOWLAND AND BAKER ISLAND AND ALL REPORTED COMMERCIAL
CRAFT OVER LARGE AREA FAMILIAR WITH SITUATION AND ONLY ALERT BOTH VISUAL AND RADIO PERIOD ZONE TIME PLUS ELEVEN AND
ONE HALF UNQUOTE 172Ø   .....(TOR 1114 NAVY 4 VO)

Form 2446
TREASURY DEPARTMENT
U. S. Coast Guard
Ed. Sept. 1930

U. S. COAST GUARD

OFFICIAL DISPATCH

UNIT HEADQUARTERS   DATE   5 JULY 1937

INCOMING HEADING

Z QUAH V NRUI Q QUAC P GR 482

FROM

ITASCA

Fleet Comdt.
Aviation
Comdt's Office
Communication Dept.
Engineer-in-Chief
Finance
Inspection
Intelligence
Law

Auditor
Personnel Board
Personnel
Procurement &
Supplies
Public Relations

TO (FOR ACTION)

HEADQUARTERS

ACKNOWLEDGE	
PRIORITY	X
ROUTINE	
NITE	

TO (FOR INFORMATION)

SAN FRANCISCO DIV.

ACKNOWLEDGE	
PRIORITY	X
ROUTINE	
NITE	

TEXT

8004 FOLLOWING TEXT MESSAGES RECEIVED BY ITASCA FROM EARHART MORNING
2 JULY ZONE ELEVEN AND ONE HALF TIME PERIOD FORWARDED FOR HEADQUARTERS
RELEASE TO ASSOCIATED AND OTHER PRESSES PERIOD ALL MESSAGES VOICE ON
3105 KILOCYCLES PERIOD ANY PRESS RELEASE SHOULD CLEARLY INDICATE THAT
ITASCA WAS AT HOWLAND AS HOMING VESSEL ONLY IN AND THAT THIS WITH WEATHER
WAS SOLE RADIO DUTY REQUESTED BY EARHART PERIOD SHIP MET ALL EARHART
REQUESTS WITH EXCEPTION INABILITY TO SECURE EMERGENCY RADIO BEARING ON
3105 KILOCYCLES DUE BRIEF EARHART TRANSMISSIONS AND USE VOICE PERIOD
WITH EXCEPTION 0803 MESSAGE NO ITASCA MESSAGE OR REQUEST ACKNOWLEDGED
BY EARHART PERIOD EARHART APPARENTLY NEVER RECEIVED ITASCA REQUESTS
TRANSMIT ON 500 KILOCYCLES IN ORDER ITASCA CUT HER IN WITH SHIP DIRECTION
FINDER 0245 RECOGNIZED EARHART VOICE MESSAGE NOT CLEAR EXCEPT QUOTE
CLOUDY WEATHER CLOUDY UNQUOTE 0345 QUOTE ITASCA FROM EARHART ITASCA
BROADCAST ON 3105 KILOCYCLES ON HOUR AND HALF HOUR REPEAT BROADCAST ON
3105 KILOCYCLES ON HOUR AND HALF HOUR OVERCAST UNQUOTE 0453 HEARD EARHART
VOICE SIGNALS UNREADABLE WITH FIVE LISTENING 0512 QUOTE WANT BEARINGS
ON 3105 KILOCYCLES ON HOUR WILL WHISTLE IN MICROPHONE UNQUOTE 0515
QUOTE ABOUT 200 MILES OUT UNQUOTE WHISTLED BRIEFLY IN MICROPHONE
0545 QUOTE PLEASE TAKE BEARING ON US AND REPORT IN HALF HOUR I WILL
MAKE NOISE IN MICROPHONE ABOUT 100 MILES OUT U NQUOTE 0730 QUOTE WE MUST
BE ON YOU BUT CANNOT SEE YOU BUT GAS IS RUNNING LOW HAVE BEEN UNABLE
REACH YOU BY RADIO WE ARE FLYING AT 1000 FEET UNQUOTE 0757 QUOTE WE
ARE CIRCLING BUT CANNOT SEE ISLAND HMRRXXOHXX CANNOT HEAR YOU GO AHEAD
ON 7500 KCS WITH LONG COUNT EITHER NOW OR ON SCHEDULE TIME ON HALF HOUR
UNQUOTE 0803 EARHART CALLING ITASCA WE RECEIVED YOUR SIGNALS BUT UNABLE TO
GET MINIMUM PLEASE TAKE BEARINGS ON US AND ANSWER ON 3105 KCS UNQUOTE
EARHART MADE LONG DASHES FOR BRIEF PERIOD BUT EMERGENCY HIGH FREQUENCY
DIRECTION FINDER COULD NOT CUT HER IN ON 3105 KCS 0844 EARHART CALLED.
ITASCA QUOTE WE ARE ON THE LINE OB POSITION 157 DASH 337 WILL REPEAT THIS
MESSAGE ON 6210 KCS WE ARE NOW RUNNING NORTH AND SOUTH UNQUOTE NOTHING
FURTHER HEARD FROM EARHART ON 6210 OR OTHER FREQUENCIES PERIOD HIGH
FREQUENCY DIRECTION FINDER ON HOWLAND WAS SET UP AS AN ADDITIONAL EMERGENCY
CAUTION WITHOUT EARHARTS REQUEST OR KNOWLEDGE PERIOD ITASCA HAD IT MANNED
THROUGHOUT NIGHT BUT NEVER ABLE TO SECURE BEARING S DUE TO EARHART VERY
BEEBRIEF TRANSMISSIONS AND HER USE OF VOICE PERIOD EARHART ADVISEED 28 JUNE
ITASCA DIRECTION FINDER FREQUENCY RANGE 550 TO 270 KILOCYCLES PERIOD ITASCA
SHIP DIRECTION FINDER MANNED AT 0725 AND EARHART REPEATEDLY REQUEST TO
TRANSMIT ON 500 KCS TO ENABLE SHIP TO CUT HER IN PERIOD SHE NEITHER
ACKNOWLEDGED NOR COMPLIED THOUGH OUR ADVICE INDICATES HER ABILITY TO
TRANSMIT ON 500 KCS PERIOD COMMUNICATIONS MONITORED THROUGHOUT BY LIEUTENANT
COMMANDER BAKER LIEUTENANT COMMANDER KENNER ENSIGN SUTTER AND LIEUTENANT
COOPER US ARMY AIR CORPS 1900

Form 8006
TREASURY DEPARTMENT
U. S. Coast Guard
Ed. Sept. 1989

SOS
AE
6 July

U. S. COAST GUARD

OFFICIAL DISPATCH

DATE 6 JULY 37

UNIT HEADQUARTERS

INCOMING HEADING

R 2 GREAT LAKES ILL JULY 5TH

FROM

COMDT NINTH NAVAL DISTRICT

TO (FOR ACTION)		ACKNOWLEDGE	
OPNAV	XX	PRIORITY.	
		ROUTINE	
		NITE	
TO (FOR INFORMATION)		ACKNOWLEDGE	
		PRIORITY	
		ROUTINE	
		NITE	

TEXT

2006 FOLLOWING UNCONFIRMED REPORT FROM MRS YOUNG WILMETTE ILLINOIS
UNIDENTIFIED PARTY WHO CLAIMS TO HAVE RECEIVED IT VIA SHORT WAVE
VOICE AT ABOUT MIDNIGHT QUOTE FROM AMELIA EARHART WE CANNOT LAST
MORE THAN THREE HOURS LONGER POSITION 42 MILES NORTH HOWLAND
ISLAND UNQUOTE SOURCE BEING CHECKED 0030

Asst Comdt.	Mail & Files
Operations	Operations
Office	Ordnance
	Permanent Board
	Public

TOR 0103 NAVY NR 2 BL.

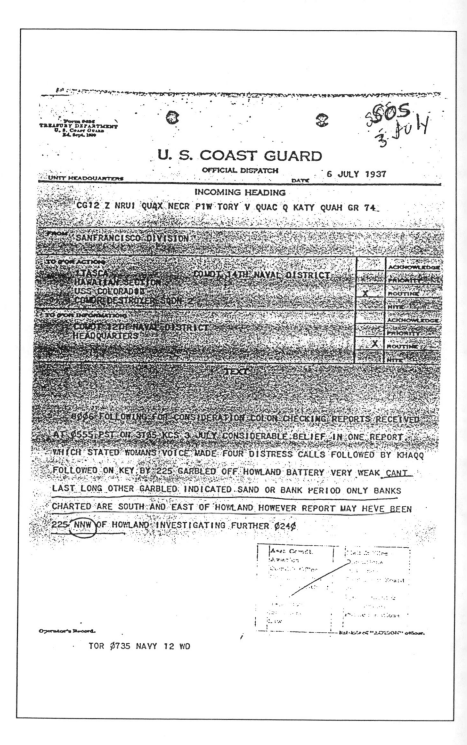

Form 0835
TREASURY DEPARTMENT
U. S. Coast Guard
24. Sept. 1929

3805
3 JULY

U. S. COAST GUARD

OFFICIAL DISPATCH

UNIT HEADQUARTERS   DATE   6 JULY 1937

INCOMING HEADING

CG12 Z NRUI QUAX NECR P1W TORY V QUAC Q KATY QUAH GR 74

FROM: SANFRANCISCO DIVISION

TO FOR ACTION		ACKNOWLEDGE	
ITASCA	COMDT 14TH NAVAL DISTRICT	PRIORITY	
HAWAIIAN SECTION		ROUTINE	X
USS COLORADO		NITE	
COMDR DESTROYER SQDN 2			

TO FOR INFORMATION		ACKNOWLEDGE	
COMDT 12TH NAVAL DISTRICT		PRIORITY	
HEADQUARTERS		ROUTINE	X
		NITE	

TEXT

8005 FOLLOWING FOR CONSIDERATION COLON CHECKING REPORTS RECEIVED AT 0555 PST ON 3105 KCS 3 JULY CONSIDERABLE BELIEF IN ONE REPORT WHICH STATED WOMANS VOICE MADE FOUR DISTRESS CALLS FOLLOWED BY KHAQQ FOLLOWED ON KEY BY 225 GARBLED OFF HOWLAND BATTERY VERY WEAK CANT LAST LONG OTHER GARBLED INDICATED SAND OR BANK PERIOD ONLY BANKS CHARTED ARE SOUTH AND EAST OF HOWLAND HOWEVER REPORT MAY HEVE BEEN 225 NNW OF HOWLAND INVESTIGATING FURTHER 0240

Asst Comdt.
Aviation
Comm. Officer

Operator's Record.

TOR 0735 NAVY 12 WO

Form 9425
TREASURY DEPARTMENT
U. S. COAST GUARD
Ed. Sept. 1930

U. S. COAST GUARD

OFFICIAL DISPATCH

UNIT HEADQUARTERS   DATE 6 JULY 1937

INCOMING HEADING

CG22KD Z QUAH V NRUI P GR 47

FROM

ITASCA

TO (FOR ACTION)				
				ACKNOWLEDGE
HEADQUARTERS			X	PRIORITY
				ROUTINE
				NITE
TO (FOR INFORMATION)				ACKNOWLEDGE
				PRIORITY
				ROUTINE
				NITE

TEXT

0805 FOR SECRETARY MORGENTHAU QUOTE INTERCEPTS OF RAGGED

TRANSMISSION INDICATE POSSIBILITY EARHART PLANE STILL AFLOAT

TWO EIGHTY ONE MILES NORTH HOWLAND STOP BEARINGS RADIO DIRECTION

FINDER ON HOWLAND CONFIRMED APPROXIMATE POSITION WE WILL ARRIVE

INDICATED POSITION THIS AFTERNOON ABOUT 1700 PLUS ELEVEN AND

ONE HALF TIME 0640

Operator's Record.   Initials of "ACTION" officer.

TOR 1335 NAVY 22 WD

U. S. COAST GUARD

OFFICIAL DISPATCH

SEARCH

UNIT HEADQUARTERS

DATE 6 JULY 37

INCOMING HEADING

WUSK V KATY Z QUAX NRUI TORY NECR P1W QUAH KATY V QUAC GR 145

FROM

SANFRANCISCO DIV

TO (FOR ACTION)

HAWAIIAN SECTION
ITASCA
COLORADO
SWAN 12 AND 14TH NAV DISTS
CGU DES SQDRN 2

TO (FOR INFORMATION)

ACKNOWLEDGE	
PRIORITY	
ROUTINE	X
NITE	
ACKNOWLEDGE	
PRIORITY	
ROUTINE	
NITE	

TEXT

8006 FOLLOWING FROM PUTNAM QUOTE PLEASE NOTE ALL RADIO BEARINGS THUS FAR OBTAINED ON EARHART PLANE APPROXIMATELY INTERSECT IN PHOENIX ISLAND REGION SOUTHEAST OF HOWLAND ISLAND PERIOD FURTHER LINE OF POSITION GIVEN BY NOONAN IF BASED ON HOWLAND WHICH APPARENTLY REASONABLE ASSUMPTION G ALSO PASSES THROUGH ISLANDS PERIOD BELIEVE NAVIGATOR AFTER OBTAINING SUCH LINE NATURALLY WOULD FOLLOW IT TO NEAREST INDICATED LAND PERIOD ADDITIONALLY IF MESSAGE STATING POSITION 281 MILES NORTH OF HOWLAND ACTUALLY WAS QUOTE SOUTH UNQUOTE INSTEAD OF NORTH ALSO INDICATES SAME REGION PERIOD WEATHER ANALYSIS INDICATES LIKELIHOOD HEADWINDS ALOFT MUCH STRONGER THAN NOONAN RECKOND WITH PROBABILITY NEVER GOT 100 MILES FROM HOWLAND AS THEY THOUGHT PERIOD LOCKHEED ENGINEERS STATE POSITIVELY PLANE COULD NOT OPERATE ITS RADIO UNLESS ON SHORE AND NO ISLANDS APPARENTLY EXIST NORTH OF HOWLAND

THEREFORE SUGGESTED THAT PLANES FROM COLORADO INVESTIGATE PHOENIX AREA AS PROMPTLY AS PRACTICABLE UNQUOTE 0210

Operator

Initials of "ACTION" officer.

TCR 0650 NAVY NR 10 BL

FORM FROM
TREASURY DEPARTMENT
U. S. COAST GUARD
R.I. Sept. 1930

U. S. COAST GUARD

OFFICIAL DISPATCH   DATE   6 JULY 1937

UNIT HEADQUARTERS

INCOMING HEADING
ᴠᴏ1 / /ᴏ94 /ᴠꞰ /ᴠꞐꞐ T Z CUAC V ᴿ NRUK P GR 47
FH25JL

FROM
SARANAC

TO (FOR ACTION)
SANFRANCISCO DIVISION

	ACKNOWLEDGE
X	PRIORITY
	ROUTINE
	NITE

TO (FOR INFORMATION)

	ACKNOWLEDGE
	PRIORITY
	ROUTINE
	NITE

TEXT

8006 YOUR 8006 0907 FOLLOWING RECEIVED FROM EᴅIᴋIᴋI COLONIAL
TELEGRAPH COMPANY ADDRESSED ALL STATIONS AND SHIPS AT 0620
QUOTE THE PLANE OF AMELIA EARHART HAS BEEN SIGHTED BY THE
COAST GUARD CUTTER ITASCA AND SHIP PROCEEDING TO HER RESCUE
UNQUOTE NO MENTION MADE OF HAVING PLANE ALONGSIDE 1213

WAL11 75 DL=WUX TDF OAKLAND CALIF JUL 8 859A

ADMIRAL WILLIAM LEAHY=CHIEF OF NAVAL OPERATIONS=

CAN WE ASCERTAIN POSSIBLY CONFIDENTIALLY EXACTLY WHAT
JAPANESE ARE DOING OR WILL DO STOP CERTAIN INFORMATION AND
ESPECIALLY DEDUCTIONS FROM WEATHER ANALYSIS MAKE ME EAGER
FOR SEARCH REGION WEST OF HOWLAND BETWEEN LONGITUDE 180 AND
ESPECIALLY APPROACHING GILBERT ISLAND AND GENERALLY
NORTHWESTERLY STOP STRONG WESTERLY DRIFT THAT REGION STOP
PERHAPS JAPANESE WILLING TO TACKLE THAT TERRITORY WHICH IS
DIRECTION THEIR MANDATE STOP MEANTIME OBVIOUSLY RADIO SIGN
IF AUTHENTIC SUBSTANTIATE WISDOM NAVY SEARCH SOUTHEASTWARD
PROGRESSING GRATEFULLY

= G P PUTNAM. 1248P.

FILE
R.F.C.

U. S. COAST GUARD
OFFICIAL DISPATCH

UNIT HEADQUARTERS   DATE 12 JULY 1937

INCOMING HEADING

FM FTHUNT

FROM
CG RDO FTHUNT

TO (FOR ACTION)				ACKNOWLEDGE
HEADQUARTERS				PRIORITY
				ROUTINE
				NITE
TO (FOR INFORMATION)				ACKNOWLEDGE
				PRIORITY
				ROUTINE
				NITE

TEXT

FOLLOWING INTERCEPTED BY FTHUNT RADIO FROM NPM(NAVAL RADIO
HONOLULU) TO P1W(COMDR DESTROYER SQDN 2)

FRANK FREEDS WHO LIVES ABOUT 2Ø MILES EAST OF YREKA CALIF STATES
THAT HE HEARD VOICE SIGNALS LAST FRIDAY NITE SOMETIME AAA AAA AND
DAWN COMING FROM THE EARHART PLANE AND RECOGNIZED THE VOICE OF
EMILIA HAVING HEARD IT BEFORE PERIOD SHE SAID THAT PLANE ON
REEF AAA AAA MILES DIRECTLY SOUTH OF HOWLAND AND THAT BOTH WERE
OK PLANE HAD ONE WING BROKEN UNQUOTE

(AAA- PARTS MSG COULD NOT COPY DUE TO STATIC AND FADING SIGNALS
(FTHUNT SAID THOUGHT IT WAS 2ØØ MILES DIRECTLY ETC. BUT FADED AT
THAT PART AND WAS NOT CERTAIN)

Operator's Record.
        TOR Ø433 FH WO

Initials of "ACTION" officer.

July 12, 1937

R. F. C.

U. S. Coast Guard
1512 H Street, N.W.
Washington, D. C.

Gentlemen:

I cannot longer refrain from telling you of the experiences we are having in connection with Miss Earhart. Something was said over the radio one morning last week by Edwin C. Hill, reporting what some medium in California had said Q and doubtless much has been said along this line, clairvoyance, which would be bungled as some of the radio messages — these things are to be expected.

I have a friend with whom I have been working for more than a year and we never make anything public — we are not ready, and have no desire for publicity, in fact would resent it, but we feel so deeply about this, so much is at stake, and we have been pleaded with to tell it, that I am giving it to you. Some day this will be a means of communication, even a hardboiled scientist as Dr. Alexis Carrel has made that statement, that he is convinced that there are men and women whose minds can travel in time as easily as we travel in space. This woman is one of such gifted people and some day she will be known for it. If Miss Earhart's conscious mind could produce to her subconscious or spirit mind it would be wonderful. There are people now who can do this and if she could, all would be well, or it would have been well earlier — they are desperately exhausted now. She of course does not know we had any spiritual or supernatural communication with her.

Without going into whether you believe in clairvoyance or supernatural communication, I'm giving you what we have. For three different times now we have heard and "seen". The diagram is the way it appears to my friend and the description we have heard. The direction from Miss Earhart herself the first night and on Saturday night was "forty miles south of the Equator — there are many, many islands about us". We are in a deep rock cove, where no ship could ever reach us....no plane would see us without flying very low — tell them where we are — dont leave us, for God's sake help us. " She repeated "We are 40 miles south of the Equator; hurry; very tired; alive; alive; dont fail us. Tell my husband alive, so weak and tired; no food, no water".

I asked if she could tell the latitude and longitude and on two different times she said"two hours thirty minutes" — 40 miles south of the Equator,"kept repeating that". I asked if they had anything to signal with and if they had food and water.

"Only . . .. tablets.....and dow we catch on ....little rubber..... - have only jacket. /..so tired. No water -tongues parched.

      I asked where the plane was and she said " do not.... know have nothing". Her voice was terribly pathetic and heart breaking to listen too - it is awful to listen to. When we first had this communication we had no idea of telling anyone - for we know what the public thinks of such things, but we were urged and begged to do so.

      And what harm could it be to ask the Itasca to have the planes search for such place as is described and now wonderful if it is correct. If only it is not now too late. She was alive this morning but we could not reach her - too weak. As I came down to work I read the papers saying the Lexington pilots would not go out perhaps until Tuesday. My heart was terrified at that because haste is so desperately needed.

      All yesterday and this morning the planes have been searching and as the old Indian guide prayed "Oh, Heavenly Father do Thou open the eyes of those who search for the sister and her companion that they may find the place where they are and oh, merciful Father we ask that Thou would comfort them, relieve their tortured suffering. Give this sister the power to see that she may help them." Maybe by this time they know something. Once Miss Earhart said she had seen the planes flying over and she shouted with all the strength she had. And how tragic if they have flown over her and have not seen her.

      We have had such amazing and wonderful experiences in this line that I am moved to tell you of this one. Perhaps some day there will be human radios and now unbelievable things done.

           Sincerely,

           Frances Folsom

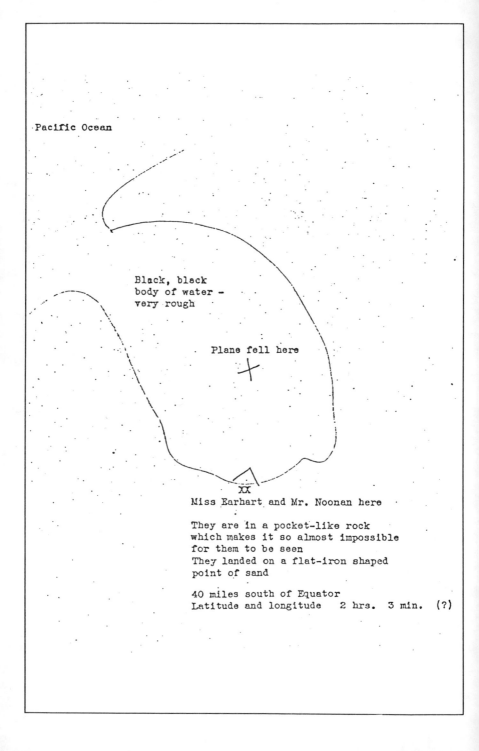

Pacific Ocean

Black, black
body of water –
very rough

Plane fell here

Miss Earhart and Mr. Noonan here

They are in a pocket-like rock
which makes it so almost impossible
for them to be seen
They landed on a flat-iron shaped
point of sand

40 miles south of Equator
Latitude and longitude   2 hrs. 3 min. (?)

DEPARTMENT OF THE NAVY
OFFICE OF THE CHIEF OF NAVAL OPERATIONS
WASHINGTON 25, D. C.

IN REPLY REFER TO
OP-921D4F/dlh
Ser 02491P92

8 FEB 1965

From: Director of Naval Intelligence
To: U.S. Department of Interior
    Office of Territories
    Attn: MRS. RUTH G. VAN CLEVE, Director
    Washington 25, D. C.

Subj: Amelia Earhart PUTNAM

Ref: (a) U. S. Dept. of Interior, Office of Territories, Washington 25, D. C.
         ltr of 1 February 1965

Encl: (1) ONI Case History File of Amelia Earhart PUTNAM

1. Enclosure (1) is forwarded for your information pursuant to your
request of 1 February 1965.

2. The nature of the information forwarded herewith is such that its
existence, source, and content, including the names of all informants, must
be carefully safeguarded. It shall be shown only to those persons whose
official duties require access thereto. If the enclosure covers an investigation of an individual, the information shall not be shown to the subject,
nor shall Naval Intelligence or any other contributing agency be mentioned
in connection with any action taken on the basis of the information. This
material is not to be forwarded outside of the control of the addressee, nor
shall any portion of the enclosed material be reproduced or removed from
this file.

3. Return of this material within thirty (30) days is requested. It should
be returned directly to the Director of Naval Intelligence (Op-921) by
endorsement, or by separate letter, reflecting cognizance of and any action
taken based on this information.

L. K. JORDAN
By direction

Bibliography

Burke, John. *Winged Legend*. New York: G. P. Putnam's Sons, 1970.

Crowl, Philip. *The U. S. Army in WW II: The War In The Pacific (Campaign in the Marianas)*. Washington D. C.: Office of the Chief of Military History, Department of the Army, 1959.

Devine, Thomas E. *Eyewitness: The Amelia Earhart Incident*. Frederick, Colorado: Renaissance House Publishing, 1987.

Goerner, Fred G. *The Search for Amelia Earhart*. Garden City, New York: Doubleday, 1966.

Joseph, Alice, MD, and Veronica Murray, MD. *Chamarros and Carolinians of Saipan - Personality Studies*. Westport, Connecticut: Greenwood Press, 1951.

Klaas, Joe and Joseph Gervais. *Amelia Earhart Lives*. New York: McGraw Hill, 1970.

Loomis, Vincent. *Amelia Earhart: The Final Story*. New York: Random House, 1985.

Meyers, Robert. *Stand By To Die*. Pacific Grove, California: Lighthouse Writers Guild, 1985.

Nevin, David. *The American Touch In Micronesia*. New

York: W. W. Norton & Co., 1977.

Price, Willard. *America's Paradise Lost*. New York: The John Day Co., 1966.

Ranney, Austin, and Howard Penniman. *Democracy In The Islands: The Micronesian Plebisites of 1983*. Washington, D.C.: American Enterprise Institute for Public Policy Research, 1985.

Reischauer, Edwin. *The Japanese*. Cambridge: Harvard University Press, 1977.

Strippel, Dick. *Amelia Earhart, The Myth and Reality*. New York: Exposition Press, 1972.

Wenkam, Robert, and Byron Baker. *Micronesia, The Breadfruit Revolution*. Honolulu: University Press of Hawaii, 1971.

Yanahari, Tadao. *Pacific Islands Under Japanese Mandate*. Oxford University Press, 1940.

INDEX

-F-

FDR. *See* Roosevelt, Franklin D., President
Flying prao (outrigger canoe) 80
Forecast, weather 20, 43
Freedom Of Information Act 16, 34

-G-

Garapan Prison 114, 116, 123 - 125, 154
Gervais, Joe 7, 8, 37
Goerner, Fred 7, 8, 36 - 37, 66 - 67, 151

-H-

Harris, Michael 64 - 65, 66, 68 - 70, 79, 80, 82, 83, 110
Heinie, John 88 - 92, 107
Howland Island 17 - 18, 19 - 21, 35
Huntoon, Dick 10 - 14, 65, 66 - 67, 70, 140 - 143

-I-

Intelligence, military 32
Iroij 74
Iroij Laplap 74
Itasca 18, 20 - 21, 35, 44, 58 - 59

-J-

Jack, Lotan 92 - 93
Jaluit 32, 89, 91, 92, 93, 94, 96, 97, 98, 104, 105, 107, 140, 154
Jibambam, Eliu 81 - 82

-K-

Kabua, Amata, President 6 - 7, 73 - 76
Kabua, Kabua, Judge 5
Kamoi 56, 107
Kempeitai 88
KHAQQ 20, 21, 59
Klaas, Joe 7
Koshu 1 - 2, 56, 83
Kwajalein 89, 93, 105, 107

T.C. "Buddy" Brennan is a Houston businessman, involved in real estate investments since
1959. A graduate of Texas A & M University, he
served in both World War II and the Korean
War, the latter as a First Lieutenant in the
Army Corps of Engineers. He is married, with
two grown children. His son, Attorney T.C.
Brennan III, has been a key figure in Buddy's
investigation into the Amelia Earhart matter.

Writer Ray Rosenbaum is retired in Springfield, Missouri, after a career in the U.S. Air Force. He flew B-17 missions over Germany in World War II and saw action in Korea and Vietnam. His early flight training was in aircraft very similar to that flown by Amelia Earhart, and he later flew C-130 transports over many of the same routes Earhart followed on her last flight. Writing is a recent second career for Rosenbaum and **WITNESS TO THE EXECUTION** is his first work of non-fiction. He is pictured here in vintage World War II gear during his flight training.